D0054004

Afrocentricity

Molefi Kete Asante

Africa World Press, Inc.

P.O. Box 1892
Trenton, New Jersey 08607

Africa World Press, Inc.
P.O. Box 1892
Trenton, N.J. 08607

New Revised Edition 1988
Second Printing 1989
Third Printing 1990
Fourth Printing 1991

Cover Design by Ife Nii-Owoo

Typeset by TypeHouse of Pennington, Inc.

Library of Congress Catalog Card Number: 87-72779

ISBN: 0-86543-067-5   Paper $9.95

Contents

Acknowledgements

Every book is autobiographical. This one is no exception inasmuch as the influences which have made this book have occurred in many parts of the world and have come through many people. I am most indebted to Kariamu Welsh, choreographer, poet, and writer, who spent many hours listening and debating these ideas with me. Indeed many of her ideas have found their way into this book without any specific reference. To her and all sisters who learn from her consciousness of victory, I say, me da ase, literally this thank you means in Twi, "I will lie at your feet."

Foreword

The need for an Afrocentric philosophy is so great that it is impossible for me not to insist on every black person reading this book. Historically, it is without precedent, combining the elements of philosophy, science, history, and mythology to give us the clearest perspective on that peculiar and particular group of people called the African-American.

The question most often encountered is why? Why the need for an Afrocentric philosophy? Why should Africa be at the center? And my question is why not? Who else would you want to have at your center? Africa belongs to an African or African-American or African Brazilian. It does not take away from the universality or humanity of man to have a particular culture or history to stand as one's center since all cultures share certain universal traits; but, they do not necessarily resemble each other. Afrocentricity resembles the black man, speaks to him, looks like him, and wants for him what he wants for himself.

Dr. Asante's book on Afrocentricity is the next step in a victorious consciousness. It is an answer to the intellectual black who wants to know why and analyze, it is the answer to the pragmatic black who wants to know where is the ritual and the support system and whose God will I be worshipping. It gives the answer to the man and woman, the twin spirits of yestercenturies, Isis and Osiris, Mawu and Lisa that we must quickly return to our centers for peace in our families.

Like David Walker, Nat Turner, Marcus Garvey, Elijah Muhammad, Molefi K. Asante is a visionary and revolutionary in his thought. Like Frederick Douglass, W.E.B. DuBois, Edward Blyden and Malcolm X, Molefi

K. Asante is articulate and resolute in his belief. Like Karenga, Madhubuti, Baraka, Asante is a living poet, still talking after everyone has shut up. But, like no one else, Dr. Asante has fused a scientific notion (the bicameral mind) with the spirit (godforce) with the historical (Africa) and the present (techdultural, African-American) to formulate a philosophy that allows for questions and analysis and provides answers and actualization.

Afrocentricity leaves no one out. Nija clearly speaks to the brother and sister who have read Siddhartha, Gibran, I Ching, Bagavadgita and said beautiful, but where is the book that reflects me?

It is that time when we must recognize all that has gone before us and all that is to come upon us. The time that is here is to be used with wisdom and foresight. Afrocentricity will aid us on the path to our center and challenge the next generation to further scholarship and spirituality.

The eyes of the world are on the African-American. The eyes of the African-American must be on his own center, one that reflects and resembles him and speaks to him in his own language. These are imperatives that the African-Americans must address, these are the issues that Molefi K. Asante has confronted and has come out looking quite like himself and 100 million of us strong here in the diaspora. It is pleasing to see one's reflection magnified 100 million times saying the right think, knowing the right way, and praising the right God.

Afrocentricity is pro-African and consistent in its beliefs that technology belongs to the world; Afrocentricity is African genius and African values created, reconstructed, and derived from our history and experiences in our best interests. If one understands properly African history, an assumption can never be made that Afrocentricity is a back to "anything" movement. It is an uncovering of one's true self, it is the pinpointing of one's center, and it is the clarity and focus through which black people must see the world in order to escalate. Maintenance and survival are no longer adequate terminology to pass on to the next generation. Our presence in the future is undisputed, but maintenance nor survival will insure our propriety or prominence. Afrocentricity is a concern for some, a possibility for others, and an imperative for the Africans of the world.

There is a Xhosa saying that "once one has had a vision, he cannot return it." Dr. Asante has had the vision and delivered the mandate. All of us who share in this vision can no longer ignore or turn our backs on it. Our center has always been there, it is our reality that is in question and once we accept that our center is the only reality, then we can have the consciousness of victory that is so necessary to be the "victor."

Kariamu Welsh

Preface

Afrocentricity is presented here in a revised and enlarged third edition. Since it first appeared in 1980, it has been revised to incorporate more Pan-African examples. However, the book emerges from the experiences of African Americans and, therefore, finds most of its examples from that history.

The centrality of the classical African civilizations in African reconstruction has been underscored by the work of the Association for the Study of Classical African Civilization. After the publication of *Afrocentricity* ASCAC came into existence as the brainchild of Jacob Carruthers and Maulana Karenga who believed that the centerpiece of Afrocentric theory was a reconnection, in our minds, of Egypt to Africa. ASCAC's development is integral to the assertive challenge Afrocentricity makes to non-African and anti-African perspectives because the Association is committed to a historiography that re-writes Africans to the classical periods.

The late Senegalese activist scientist, Cheikh Anta Diop, is the most prominent figure in this movement for the anteriority of Egypt. The re-naming of the University of Dakar as Université de Cheikh Anta Diop is a principled Afrocentric statement that represents honor to the profound influence Diop had on African scholars.

Cheikh, as some of us often called him, had protégés, students, and disciples both inside and outside of Senegal. Habib Sy, the Afrocentric communicationist, and Diao Ba, the Afrocentric physicist, represent in their own research interests the great range of Diop's scholarship.

Afrocentricity, as philosophy, claims Cheikh Anta Diop as one of its earliest pioneers because he re-constructed African cultural theory with Africa as subject. Beyond his detailed descriptions and analyses of African societies and languages, he showed that Europe and Asia were but junior variations on the original African theme in philosophy and science. He embodied Afrocentric scholarship.

Cheikh was able to publish his earlier works because of the creativity of Alioune Diop, the founder of *Presence Africaine*.

And now the torch is passed. Each generation sees a little more through the cocoon, and each generation reclaims a little more of the history and culture.

The marks of the truly Afrocentric personality are intelligence and boldness, one without the other is mere showmanship. Intelligence manifested in an acute awareness of self, perception of others, and the universe from an Afrocentric perspective is a motivator but it is not enough by itself. With boldness, which is not cockedness or aggression, but Afrocentric assertion, intelligence becomes intellectual activism. To assert without intelligence is force but it is never seen as power until it is coupled with intelligence.

This generations' battle-cry is no different from that of previous generations. The aim and the spirit are the same. We walk the way of a new level of freedom. We seek to no longer be victimized by others as to our place in the center of world history. We do this not because of arrogance but because it is necessary to place Africa at the center of our existential reality, else we will remain detached, isolated, and spiritually lonely people in societies which constantly bombard us with anti-Africa rhetoric and symbols, sometimes from Africans themselves who have been trained by the enemies of Africa.

Chapter 1
The Essential Grounds

Perspective

This book offers a philosophical inquiry into the future of the Afrocentric perspective and a testament of Nija, the ideology of victorious thought.

Afrocentricity is the centerpiece of human regeneration. To the degree that it is incorporated into the lives of the millions of Africans on the continent and in the Diaspora, it will become revolutionary. It is purposeful, giving a true sense of destiny based upon the facts of history and experience. The psychology of the African without Afrocentricity has become a matter of great concern. Instead of looking out from one's own center, the non-Afrocentric person operates in a manner that is negatively predictable. The person's images, symbols, lifestyles, and manners are contradictory and thereby destructive to personal and collective growth and development. Unable to call upon the power of ancestors, because one does not know them; without an ideology of heritage, because one does not respect one's own prophets; the person is like an ant trying to move a large piece of garbage only to find that it will not move.

It takes no great gift to be able to identify the symbols which will, in their completeness, transform the whole of the African world and necessarily influence European and Asian thought. No longer are we looking whitely through a tunnel lit with the artificial beams of Europe; we now are able to experience the Afrocentricity that the great prophets Garvey, DuBois, Fanon, Nkrumah, Muhammad, Malcolm, and Karenga had predicted for us. Afrocentricity takes a simulsense form once it is a fact in one's life; it is not linear, cannot be analyzed in a single line, and is inherently circular. I speak of it as a transforming agent in which all things that were old become new and a transformation of attitudes, beliefs, values, and behavior results. It becomes everywhere sensed and is everywhere present. A new reality is invoked; a new vision is introduced. In fact, it is the first and only reality for African people; it is simply rediscovery. Our eyes become new or rather what we see becomes clearer.

There is first suggested the existence of an African Cultural System; then the juxtaposition of African and American ways; and finally the values derived from the African-American experience. In a very positive sense, we have the range of African-American definitions and values within this statement and it becomes necessary to explore the manifestations of our cultural values both in their contemporaneity and potentiality. Unquestionably on the Continent our cultural system is manifested in diverse ways as it is in the Diaspora. We have one African Cultural System manifested in diversities. Nevertheless to speak of the Arab of Algeria as my brother is quite different from speaking so of the African-Brazilian, Cuban or Nigerian. We respond to the same rhythms of the universe, the same cosmological sensibilities, the same general historical reality as the African descended people. Indeed, Shango, Ogun, Oshun, and Obatala have meaning for us even if it is only at the essential level of symbol. All African people participate in the African Cultural System although it is modified according to specific histories and nations. In this way, we know that Yoruba, Asante, Wolof, Ewe, Nuba, and African-Americans possess values and beliefs derived from their own particular histories yet conforming to the African Cultural System. All cultural systems are responsive to the environment; ours is no different but it is better for us because it is derived from our own historical experiences while maintaining fidelity in its best form to the African Cultural System (Asante, 1987).

Adoption of Islam is as contradictory to the Diasporan Afrocentricity as Christianity has been. Christianity has been dealt with admirably by other writers, notably Karenga; but Islam within the African-American community ha yet to come under Afrocentric scrutiny. Understand that this oversight is due more to a sympathetic audience than it is to the perfection of Islam for African-Americans. While the Nation of Islam under the leadership of Elijah Muhammad was a transitional nationalist movement, the present emphasis of Islam in America is more cultural and religious. This is a serious and perhaps tragic mistake; because apart from its historical contradictions, there exists monumental contradictions in its application. All religions rise out of the deification of someone's nationalism. Understand this and you will discern the key to our own victory. Afrocentrists understand and appreciate the transforming power of Islam and indeed recognize that same power within Christianity, Judaism, Buddhism, Hinduism, and Marxism. It is no mystery; in fact, it is predictable that there should be transforming and energizing force in all religions. Islam has no distinction except in the specific history which has been deified. How has it been deified for the world? What are its assumptions and parameters? Whose history and culture are held up as the standard? What are the forces at work within the religion?

Putting these questions already causes you to contemplate the extent of the deification of the history. Islam, as an organized religion, had its origin in the Arabian desert, somewhere in the vicinity of Mecca and Medina, depending upon where one wants to place the emphasis of Muhammad's life. Without begging the question by asserting that Islam is older than Muhammad, consider that such a posture has been taken by all religions when assailed for having a place and time or origin. Buddhists will say that Buddhism existed before Gotama; Christians will says that Christianity existed before Jesus; and Jews will say that Judaism existed before Moses. This is all true because the elements which are necessary for effective human living and collective group consciousness existed before any of these individual people. By the same token, Afrocentrists will say that *Nija* existed before Asante's *Afrocentricity* or Welsh's *Mfundalai*. They will be correct to assert such a position. Nevertheless, the truth of the matter is that the statement of the position must begin somewhere, in someplace with someone. Islam had such a beginning; in fact, as we know it, Islam began with Muhammad. Consequently, the initial responsibility and direction of Islam belonged to Muhammad much as the initial responsibility of Nija belongs to its originators.

The organization of Islam has been effective, not because of any more special relationship to God than any other people, but because of the genius of its early leaders. Consider the factors which have contributed to the over-powering submissiveness of Africans and other non-Arabs to the culture and religion of the Arabs. First, the language of God is said to be Arabic. Secondly, the pilgrimage must be made to Mecca. Thirdly, to pray effectively, one must turn his or her head toward Mecca. Fourthly, Muhammad is said to be the last and most important prophet. Fifthly, certain Arabizing customs are looked upon as valuable and significant, e.g., change of name to Arab name, Arab clothes, and female subordination, to name a few. Now let us consider why this is anathema to Afrocentricism and like Christianity makes us submit to a strange God.

Arabic is neither more or less significant as a language than Yoruba, Kiswahili or Ebonics; it is and should be more highly honored, however, by Arabs because it is their language. Did God or the Bicameral Mind speak to

Muhammad in Arabic? Since Muhammad was an Arab, I would expect his God to have spoken to him in his language as my God speaks to me in Ebonics and Kiswahili. There is nothing more sacred about one language than another; one language may have special significance to one people more than to others. Understand how Islam made Arabic the language of millions of non-Arabs, thus spreading the culture in a most powerful manner. To read the Koran correctly, one had to do so in Arabic. This meant that those non-Arabs who wanted to become Islamic had to go many steps further than the native born Arabs who already know the language of God. Look at the trip being run on his head! Unaware that God or the Bicameral Mind could speak to him, and probably did, in his own language; the brother ran off to learn a foreign tongue. If your God cannot speak to you in your language, then he is not your God. Your God is the God who speaks to you in your language. What is your language? It is the language with which you first got your consciousness. Thus, for African Americans, this would be Ebonics (the language of black Americans), for Yoruba, the language would be Yoruba, and, for Asante, the language would be Twi. If you want to hear your God in the language of your ancestors, then learn an African language like Kiswahili or Yoruba. I implore you with every drop of blood in my veins to severely evaluate any and every idea that is contrary to your center; learning and speaking Arabic to become more spiritual is way off center.

Why do you suppose the religion of Islam made Mecca the place of the pilgrimage? I know that the Kaaba is there, but really what is the importance of the pilgrimage to Mecca? It is politically important. For an Eskimo, a Finn, an Argentinian, or a Japanese,the pilgrimage could be extremely harsh punishment. But for Arabs? The nature of Islam is to make it more difficult for non-Arabs thereby securing their allegiance more strongly. Once a person has accepted the basic tenets and attempts to practice the religion as the Arabs, that person is in an unnatural situation because it was not meant for him. A journey to Mecca for the Arabs is natural; it is their sacred city, close to their populations, and steeped in their culture. The African who makes the pilgrimage often flies over numerous sacred cities and sites of his own to march around someone's sacred stone. Afrocentricism teaches us to honor Jamestown where the first bloods truly destined touched the American earth; to honor Thebes, the most sacred city; to honor Oshogbo where the healing waters flow; to honor Lake Bosumtwi where the God of Africa dwells; to honor the sacred spot where Nat Turner planned his revolt in Virginia. We have within our own history the most sacred and holiest places on the earth. Afrocentricism directs us to visit them and meditate on the power of our ancestors.

Turning one's head to Mecca is symbolic of the same cultural insistence which keeps the convert looking in the direction of another's culture, not his own. Since for the Afrocentric person, our God is everywhere present, this particular ritual is not understandable. Only in the sense of the Arabizing influence of the religion can it truly be understood. Do not get me wrong, it is one of the most powerful tools of mind control ever created. Suppose Afrocentrism had you and the white people of Europe and the Arabs of Arabia turning heads towards the sacred forests of Oshogbo, or towards Tuskegee, or Mount Kilimanjaro? We would have developed the instrument of collective will necessary for our victory. It is soon to some, although it will not come in terms of turning heads; it will emerge in the form of a collective consciousness capable of developing an international will and manifestation.

Islam says that *Muhammad* is the last and most important prophet. That statement is correct if you understand it in light of the deified history of the Arabs. Would the greatest nationalist who ever lived in Arabia not be considered the last and most important prophet? Understand this point, a nationalist is not necessarily a racist; indeed, the true nationalist is never a racist. Muhammad was a nationalist who strove to bring about a cohesive spirit among his people; notwithstanding the fact that his teachings were accepted by some non-Arabs. This is the case with any perfected nationalist movement. It becomes "universal" after its acceptance by those to whom it came. Adherence will come from many different places but the initial message of the nationalist is always to his people. If others want to accept such nationalist teachings, they can, so long as they adopt the behaviors, cultural habits, clothings, and lifestyles of the people from whom the words first emanated. This is why the Arabs say that Muhammad was the last and most important of the prophets; if another one comes then he must be a false prophet. In addition, this assures the stability of the religion, the power of the movement, and the honored place of the founding and final light of the national religion. Acceptance of the previous prophets is a necessary and practical action; however, such acceptance never honors the first more than the last.

The most crippling effect of Islam as well as Christianity for us may well be the adoption of non-African customs and behaviors, some of which are in direct conflict with our traditional values. We out Arab the Arabs as we have out Europeanized the Europeans from time to time. This is not so with the Afrocentrist. He or she studies every thought, action, behavior, and value, and if it cannot be found in our culture or in our history, it is dispensed with quickly. This is not done because we have something against someone else's culture; it is just not ours. We do not have too many complaints with the person who decides to accept someone else's culture, religion, or ideology, be it Islam, Christianity, or Marxism, if it serves him better than his own. However, for us it is impossible to see how anything from outside ourselves can compare with what is in our history. We have a formidable history, replete with the voice of God, the ancestors, and the prophets. Our manner of dress, behavior, walk, talk, and values are intact and workable when we are Afrocentric. Our problems come when we lost sight of ourselves, accept false doctrines, false gods, mistaken notions of what is truly in our history, and assume an individualistic, antihumanistic, and autocratic posture. Thus, we say if you must change your name, choose an African name, not an Arab name. Why go through the trouble of discarding a European name to choose an Arab one? Before the Arabs came in force into Africa with the Jihads of 640-642 A.D., few indigenous Africans had ever heard names like Muhammad, Yusef, Kareem, and Ali. These names came only with Islam. Let us be circumspect and let us be certain before we make our moves. Nat Turner taught that the most valuable lesson is certainty, and we learned from his experience that you can never be too prepared. Up from the intellectual and spiritual pit which has held our mighty people! Let each person take his post in the vanguard of this collective consciousness of Afrocentricism! Teach it! Practice it! And victory will surely come as we carry out the Afrocentric mission to humanize the Universe.

Afrocentricity is the belief in the centrality of Africans in post modern history. It is our history, our mythology, our creative motif, and our ethos exemplifying our collective will. On basis of our story, we build upon the work of our ancestors who gave signs toward our humanizing function. *Nija* teaches in quarter 4, verse 4, "You are meant to be a sign for the world." The songs, poems, stories, sermons, and proverbs demonstrate our ancestors inexorable movement toward the humanizing function, more fitted by a higher civilization, a peaceful agrarian mythology, and spiritual explorations, our people affirm in the Diaspora and on the continent the mission of spirit.

Afrocentricity does not convert you by appealing to hatred or lust or greed or violence. As the highest, most conscious ideology, it makes its points, motivates its adherents, and captivates the cautious by the force of its truth. You are its ultimate test. You test its authenticity by incorporating it into your behavior. At the apex of your consciousness, it becomes your life because everything you do, it is. As I write on this paper with black ink on white paper, I recognize the ordering power, the civilizing ability, and the intelligence of the ancestors. Formlessness becomes form; black spaces are filled with truth; and so we are like that in every respect. This, of course, is a mythic reality, but the kind of mythic reality which dictates how Afrocentricity governs every moment of any life. The Christian will tell you that since they accepted Jesus old things passed away and all things became new. What they meant is what I mean; a new perspective, a new approach, a new consciousness invades our behavior and consequently with Afrocentricity you see the movies differently, you see other people differently, you read books differently, you see politicians differently; in fact, nothing is as it was before your consciousness. Your conversion to Afrocentricity becomes total as you read, listen, and talk with others who share the collective consciousness. It supersedes any other ideology because it is the proper sanctification of your own history.

In a similar fashion to the Africans who are Christian or Muslim the brothers and sisters who take on the habits and customs of ancient Hebrews are in search of a past that stares them in the face whenever they look in a mirror. You must always begin from where you are, that is, if you are Yoruba begin with Yoruba history and mythology; if you are Kikuyu, begin with Kikuyu history and mythology; if you are African-American, begin with African-American history and mythology. Irrespective of present locations, the roots of all African people go back to East Africa, the cradle of human history. We do not find the Hebrews or those related to them until thousands of years after the ancient Egyptians (Africans) and Nubians (Africans) had appeared. If Moses were a Hebrew, he was one who appeared in history long after the dawn of human history. The African continent gave birth to Africans; this is our ultimate reality. During our reconstruction, we must not lose sight of our total Afrocentricity. It cannot develop further until we rid ourselves of all fantasies except those that grow out of our own history. Renunciation of Negroness and western influences are to be highly praised but renunciation of one slavery and the adoption of another must be declared an ideological deviation from Afrocentricity. The dispensing with symbols and scriptures which stand outside of us is a move toward national recovery.

Washingtonianism

Booker T. Washington was one of the most astute black leaders who ever lived. Few men loved their people as did Washington. His sacrifice for the educational, economic, and political advancement of his people took the greatest degree of sagacity and courage of his era. Washington's place in history has been clouded by European scholars. They wanted to demonstrate, on one hand, that a conflict of objectives existed between Washington and Du Bois, when in actuality it did not.

The differences of opinion between Washington and Du Bois were never so great as the difference between Du Bois and Garvey, yet in neither case did either of the thinkers demonstrate a goal any different than the liberation of African people. In fact, Booker T. Washington like Du Bois and Garvey, understood the African connection and attempted to exploit it for African progress (Washington, 1899). Unquestionably great men will differ, but the differences were not over ultimate objectives but tactics. An objective is the profound end rooted in the historical imperative of a people to which all Afrocentric action is directed. Tactic refers to the measures and methods employed to advance us toward our objective.

In analyzing Washington's place, the Afrocentricist must look at his intellectual growth pattern in order to determine his true character. As a young man, he made an Afrocentric commitment to the black people of Alabama. Although there may have been only a few positions for a person of Washington's training, he took the position in Alabama because of his sense of duty committing his life to the struggle for a decent education for blacks in the South. It was not only a committed act, it was courageous given the environment during this time in history. Ku Klux Klan groups had formed, lynchings were taking place regularly and Southern whites were appropriating blacks' land. This arena greeted Washington when he stepped onto the world's center. His effective management of that arena left us a memorable legacy.

What have been called accommodationist positions were often deliberate manipulations of his white audience and his positions on the legal aspirations of blacks were clear and forceful. " . . . I would not have the Negro deprived of any privilege guaranteed to him by the constitution of the United States. It is not best for the Negro that he relinquish any of his constitutional rights" (Washington, 1899). Furthermore, he argues that legislation must not confer upon an ignorant and poor white man legal and political privileges denied to the black (Washington, 1899:210).

Perhaps the Atlanta Exposition Speech was the great hallmark of his genius yet it infuriated Northern blacks who did not understand the nature of the racist South nor the legacy of slavery still prevalent in the minds and behaviors of Africans. Washington understood that legacy and attempted to squeeze the most benefit possible out of it. What he did not do to the satisfaction of Northern blacks was to attack the wolves in their home, preferring to dog them with his good sense and in feeling that the ultimate victory would come at a later date. Yet, he also failed to satisfy the white racists who wanted no part of the New South, even with "one hand as separate as the fingers." Indeed, the "one hand" disturbed them. Although Washington achieved the greatest degree of publicity for this speech in 1895 and it became his signature on the age, it cannot be called his most representative work. As in the case of all political geniuses, he had a pattern of growth which could not be contained in a single speech. Indeed the Atlanta Exposition Speech was eloquent and oratorically sculptured from the best traditions of public speaking but it was not representative of Washington's life work. His victories at the economical, political, and educational levels came about because of his commitment to excellence. A considerate view of historical realities in the 1890's and early part of the 20th Century produced in him one dynamic, dedicated, and determined African.

Washingtonianism was mainly economic independence. It was this particular aspect of Washington's program that appealed to Marcus Garvey, but economic independence could not produce freedom; indeed Washington's real mistake was not to see the indivisibility of freedom. Economic freedom must always be connected to political and cultural freedom else freedom does not truly exist. The fragility of economic independence has been demonstrated throughout the United States, Kenya, Soviet Union, Zimbabwe, Zambia, Liberia, and South Africa. In addition, even the control of production and land can be tenuous if a people do not possess the political power to safeguard their economic freedom. In fact, land must never be equated with freedom; freedom is a mental state. Furthermore, political power or state power without cultural and economic power is also meaningless for liberation. These African nations which have gained political independence but have not secured their cultural or economic independence remain enslaved to alien forces. Although Washington predicted African economic and political independence, he showed no real appreciation for cultural liberation. In his view, a confident economic posture overrode all other considerations. As a result, he is criticized by the Marxists as a capitalist and by the capitalists as a socialist. For Washington, economic independence was not an ideology; it was a practical philosophy. This program was meant to create an independent element within the black population. To this end, Tuskegee Institute was merely a base for Washington's philosophy of success. It woefully lacked Afrocentricity. The Spirit of the Age had not revealed itself in African history and culture at this time and therefore Washington shared in the ignorance of his era. Only now armed with the past, can we look to the future.

Numerous ideologues since Washington have included nuances of his philosophical postures in their works, particularly on education and economics. The reason for this is the powerful truth inherent in the Kiswahili saying, "muko vile mjiwakavyo wenyewe, si vile wengine wawawekavyo." "You are what you make of yourself, not what other make you." Washington viewed economics as developed through the power of the people themselves. This view was only shortsighted because it lacked an Afrocentric perspective which would have involved politics and culture as well as economics. Thus, its failure and the subsequent failure of other such Washingtonian ideas such as "Black Capitalism" and McKissick's "Soul City" attest not to any lack of enthusiasm but rather a lack of ideological direction. Similarly, other economic programs suffer from the same misconception of the African experience in America. Unlike some others, Washington, at least, knew the character of the people with whom he was dealing. Nevertheless, no program, however brilliantly organized, can survive if its conception is not based upon Afrocentricity. Therefore, Booker T. Washington was unable to generate the lasting spirit so essential as a revolutionary characteristic of people seeking reconstruction. He could not give what he did not possess himself.

Garveyism

Garveyism, despite the attacks and charges hurled against it until recently, was the most perfect, consistent, and brilliant ideology of liberation in the first half of the 20th Century. In no nation in the world was there a philosophical treatment of oppressed people any more creative than Garveyism. It was used as a vehicle for a people's uplift as well as a weapon against those whites and blacks who had vested interest in the status quo. Garveyism was an idea fulfilling its time. It took the common man of African descent, up-rooted from his culture, and fortified him.

Marcus Mosiah Garvey was born in St. Ann, Jamaica, on August 17, 1887, to Marcus and Sarah Garvey. From an early age, he expressed an intense desire to see the upward movement of our race. Garvey travelled to Costa Rica, Venezuela, Nicaragua, Honduras, and Columbia. In each place, he saw Africans in the worst jobs and in the poorest houses. Leaving South America, he returned to Jamaica for a brief while until he could set sail for London in 1912. In the metropolis of the British Empire, he met the stalwart Pan-African nationalist, Duse Mohammed, publisher of the *African Times and Orient Review* and later the *Comet*, based in London and Lagos, respectively. But it was reading Booker T. Washington's *Up from Slavery* that really moved Garveyism toward the U.S.A. and the creation of the Universal Negro Improvement Association. He became resolute that he must help to make the black man's nation.

By 1914, Garvey was sure that he could unite all of the black peoples of the world into one great body to establish a country and government (Garvey, 1969). His program offered these seven steps:

1. Awakening and uniting all Africans
2. Changing the thinking of the aroused to potential
3. Channeling emotional energies toward constructive racial interests
4. Mass sacrificial work
5. Through education in science and industry and character building, stress mass education
6. Prepare nationalists to run nations
7. Keep the young nations together after they were formed

These steps were rooted in Garvey's undying love for the people. He understood that the assertion and affirmation of the African cultural heritage was necessary for true liberation of Diasporan Africans.

The basic idea of Garveyism—Race Power—presents little innovation because race power had always characterized the white view of the world. Racial power had been the central idea in European thought since Bartholomew Las Casas. It dominated every major philosopher of Europe; Darwin, Wagner, Nietzsche, and even Marx. These Europeans may have differed in their conceptualizations of race power, but none questioned the central idea itself. Whether it is a biological or mechanical idea, it is a prevalent one. Consequently, Garveyism drew upon the dynamic teachings of Edward Blyden, Martin Delaney, and Bishop Henry McNeal Turner. As such, Garvey was in excellent company with the idea of race power.

Garvey's work was multi-dimensional. Although the press concentrated on the Back-to-Africa concept, it never was a central part of Garvey's program. He instituted cultural symbols which captured the essence of a nationalistic philosophy; his mind was sharp and geared to the media. As a media manipulator, growing from his years as a journalist and printer, Garvey knew how to communicate with his audience. Garveyism was a popular philosophy, understood from the least to the most sophisticated person in his audience. His sweeping images captivated the journalists who observed the movement. They seemed taken with the eloquence of his symbols and the substance of his messages.

Garvey was a Pan-Africanist. He saw clearly the relationship of Africans on the continent and in the Diaspora as variations of one people, one giant cultural project. The complete name of his organization emphasized his Pan-African commitment, the Universal Negro Improvement Association and African Communities League. Garvey was unabashedly devoted to a race first doctrine, not race only but certainly race first. As Tony Martin has shown in his brilliant works on Garvey, the complete Garvey was a Pan-African nationalist whose entire life was consumed with seeing oppressed and downtrodden Africans respected and respecting themselves.

The teleological assumptions of Garveyism are productive. Garvey sought to produce the new black man, to mold him, civilize and develop him. A strong teleological commitment drives the production of new people, organized in character-building institutions, and building nations for the future. His vision foreshadowed the Afrocentric road to self-respect and dignity. In retrospect, we we can say that Nija was the idea behind Garvey's impact on African people.

As a viewpoint, Garveyism cannot be denied since people rendered their support to his movement, and he outdistanced all of his contemporaries. Garvey made sense, common sense to the people; they went for that position because it rang true. *There are no struggles against facts, only struggles for faith.* Garvey's whole strategy was to attain an overwhelming vote of confidence from the African world. Over 10 million paid their dues and pledged allegiance to the recovery of African for Africans. What Garvey showed them and what is demonstrable today and tomorrow is that African people respond to their collective memory of the continent. Such acceptance places him into the high echelons of the holy places. Any concrete analysis of Garveyism will reveal the decisive support of powerfully nation-building symbols from us which speak to us.

Garveyism represents the prototype of mass movements generally and nationalist movements specifically. Marcus Mosiah Garvey's spirit is found in every page of nationalist development and ideology. He constructed the framework for future builders. A genius of immense proportions he may have been a university professor, a poet, a playwright, a historian or a military general; he was, however, what our history needed in a moment of crisis.

Kingism and Nonviolence

Born in 1929, Martin Luther King, Jr.'s childhood and youth paralleled the long years of lynchings and the Depression as well as the attendant problems following two world wars. During his adolescence, the United States emerged from the second European World War indebted to its African citizens who had fought bravely to defend democracy. But instead of reaping the accrued interest from that debt, African-American men and women were denied at home the very democracy they defended abroad. The wartime economy had encouraged large numbers of our people to migrate North. After the war however, the industrial shift to a peace time economy lessened the demand for cheap black labor and caused great upheavals in the labor force of which blacks had become a part. Despite this, the desire of African Americans for quality education, housing, and jobs remained unabated. Consequently, the objectives of black people met with strident racism and political apathy towards their post-war plight. Although this undercurrent for confrontation existed before he came to national attention, King became the catalyst for such a national explosion (King, 1964).

Since 1955, nonviolence and civil disobedience have become synonymous with Martin Luther King. In that year, Mrs. Rosa Parks refused to give her Montgomery, Alabama bus seat to a white man, and her defiance sparked the fires of the Civil Rights Movement. What Mrs. Parks did by her actions, King elevated to a national moral philosophy which became the catalyst for black activism of the 1960's. He redefined the limits of civil disobedience for the world and breathed new vigor into peaceful protests against entrenched racist establishments. His nonviolent philosophy coupled with active civil disobedience brought about numerous legal and social changes in America. King was the classic nonviolent activist who argued for moral force and redemptive love (King, 1964).

Few activists have galvanized the spirit of the times more than King, and as is often the case, that charisma determines who will, and who will not, appeal to the masses. King not only appealed to the masses, but his philosophical approach also raised the issue of just and unjust laws to the foreground of social change. In his "Letter From a Birmingham Jail" (1963), he defined just laws as those which were in keeping with the laws of God, and unjust laws as those which violated human dignity. He determined that to demonstrate respect for the rule of law, he and his followers had to submit to the penalty enacted by the legal system whether those laws were unjust or just. However, from an Afrocentric perspective, this aspect of King's philosophy raises several questions, one of which is the need to accept any penalty for unjust laws. This contradiction was never successfully explained in King's philosophy.

Despite its successes, the age of King was an age of contradictions within the African-American community. He saw himself standing between the apathetic and the nationalist. This was *his* principal contradiction. It became impossible for him to stand between the population and . . . unless he stood for someone else. In other words, his philosophy was a legacy of holding forth between the parts of our community rather than standing with those who rejected the hollow American promise. King viewed himself as a positive force for whites who wanted to ward off the racial prophets of nationalism, while simultaneously helping apathetic blacks toward self-discovery. The net effect, of course, was the radicalization of the apathetic, and King's own ostracization from the nationalists. Consequently, the more he stood between these opposing forces within the community, the more contradictions emerged. (Afrocentricity was only

. beginning to develop, and King was unable to project or extend the philosophical notions which radically challenged European reality.)

Despite this, the momentum of Dr. King's charisma and the timeliness of the Civil Rights Movement ushered in a host of ministeres like Jackson, Abernathy, Young, Walker, and Shuttlesworth who took up the batons of nonviolence, and led numerous marches in a hundred cities.

In the realm of philosophy, King's views were new and initially dynamic. In the realm of action, King's age made the demonstration a rhetorical instrument; and in the real of ethics, he extended the moral frame of reference. Kingism survives in a muffled form but it should be remembered as a significant action philosophy, not as an Afrocentric statement which it never claimed nor could ever claim.

Elijah Muhammad's Objectivism

Objectivism is the use of our cultural artifacts as symbols in all reproductive and creative work. Its elemental basis is in mental attitude; its expressive mode is symbolic. Without the attitude, the expression is meaningless. Objectivism is the detailed arrangement of Afrocentricity. In other words, as each person begins at his or her center and reaches outward all of the symbols of the center are extended with him. Elijah Muhammad did that better than anyone in his era. He pointed out that we had moved toward someone else's center without stopping to think of our own. He demonstrated that we are creators and producers but we have been too eager to relinquish our objects. In Africa we gave up our bodies; in America, we gave up our minds; and vice versa; both are against the interest of our victory. Elijah taught us to reclaim our total selves.

Our poets, the greatest ancestral voices among us, Guillen, Soyinka, Dunbar, Dumas, Bitek, ya Salaam, Karenga, Okai, Kariamu, Sonia, yes, Pathé, Hughes, Haki, and Baraka, know the truth of ancestral objects. They sing of coconuts and palm trees, Martin Luther King avenues and soul blues. Chaka, Dinizulu, Osei Tutu, Akhenaten, Piankhy, Tarhaka, Nzingha, Candace, Yaa Asantewa, Harriet, and Sojourner. Their words of soul spring forth from Shango; they know umbanda and can shout with the Baluba in amazement at our deep spirits. This is not all they know or can do. By extension, they are in touch with every fiber of the image of a nation contained in our people. Only with the most powerful drive toward objectivism can Afrocentricity be fully realized among us. They have kept us always from losing ourselves.

This is precisely why Elijah Muhammad's Islam was so central to our march to victory. He liberated the symbols of religion, denouncing those that had enslaved us, and provided different, more vital symbols for the

African American. Not fully conscious of the historical background of African exile in America, he knew our depraved condition. With this knowledge, this genius of a man began to effect a change in African-Americans through constant preaching against the slave mentality. The white Christian was as evil for Elijah as he had been for David Walker and Martin Delaney. Elijah felt that evil was inherent in the white race, and preached that whites could not help themselves. We know now, of course, that the condition of evil in whites is not inherent, but inherited through history and environment. Elijah assumed it was native, and proclaimed that "whites are devils." But it was by choice that whites became evil in their dealings with Africans. The social and environmental factors produced the choices that they accepted and thus it became difficult for an African in America to consider the possibility that whites could be without avarice and deviousness. Hence, whiteness symbolized evil (Maglanbayan, 1972).

Like Marcus Garvey, Elijah Muhammad was an effective organizer who readily grasped our economic realities. He knew that consumerism could not provide economic autonomy, and so he also aimed to control production. His "help yourself" program provided a brand of Islam which primarily was nationalistic, and which proved a corrective measure for the liberation of African-Americans from the years of "sleep" in the land of plenty. He unmasked the evil doers, removed the wool from our eyes, and demanded that we remake our world. Blacks learned from the Honorable Elijah that the white choice was not the right choice. Instead, he gave us Malcolm X, Muhammad Ali, and Louis Farrakhan. These messengers have come to symbolize the creative, exceptional, and powerful legacy which Elijah bequeathed to us. Indeed, he inspired a whole generation of scholarship, literature, artistic expression, and science. Elijah Muhammad made David Walker's words practical and concrete (Walker, 1965).

Du Bois

W.E.B. Du Bois stands at the helm of intellectual and political advancement in the contemporary world. He is at once brilliant, powerful, and humanistic. At no time in the present era and rarely in previous epochs has any one individual so completely dominated the intellectual landscape on matters political, social, and historical. Every treatise on urban life is incomplete without reference to Du Bois, and no successful scholarly study of the economic, legal or historical implications of slavery can be achieved without homage to Du Bois. In sociology, history, and political science, he laid the basis for contemporary analyses. Of the 2,377 articles and books in his bibliography, clearly the majority were on African and African-American issues although he covered almost every conceivable topic (Partington, 1977). Du Bois had a mind so agile that it could capture the essential elements of Washingtonianism and dispense with its non-essential ones, it could accept a Marxist interpretation of history and extend that interpretation to include racism; and could read Goethe while extoling the genius of the bards who created the spirituals.

Despite his intense love for African people, Du Bois was not Afrocentric (Du Bois, 1961:142). He studied African people not from an African perspective but from a European one which employed Eurocentric methods to analyze and study black people. Few African scholars of his era, if any, could break out of the tightness of European thought. Indeed, only Afrocentric scholars have been able to achieve that victory. Although he demonstrated admirably that the African could excel at European scholarship, this apologetic posture was necessary in his mind to establish our respectability worldwide.

Educated at the University of Berlin and at Harvard, the citadel of western images in America, Du Bois was steeped in the traditions of European scholarship. Despite this, his soul argued with the restrictions of Europe, and frequently broke from its bonds as is evident in such poems as "I Am The Smoke King" and other plaintive lamentations for a people too long asleep. Du Bois prepared the world for Afrocentricity; the protector of an idea who did not fully recognize its power but who would have shouted to see it come. Afrocentricity was the most logical end of his own brilliant growth pattern. The Soul of his Age, standing astride intellectual history, he placed one foot in Europe and the other in Africa to balance his soul and mind (Du Bois, 1971).

Du Bois' unyielding mission was the humanizing of the world through the humanizing of America. It was a difficult if not impossible task. America's ethical principles were ensnarled in competitiveness. The thrust for humanity based upon culture and spiritual values was anathema to profit and competition. In this respect, Du Bois' mission was based on false assumptions about the perfectibility of competitive profiteers who saw progress only in conflict and confrontation. His high calling as an eyewitness to human history played out on the stage of life, involved him in the most intractable of social schemes, that is, the integration of the American society. While discrimination could be minimized, redundant, and controlled, integration could hardly be dictated or programmed. Always the seer, Du Bois advanced integration as the key to human progress in America. Working from a Eurocentric vision, he participated in the philosophical currents of Western Europe, and therefore reflected the same mental flow as Darwinism, Marxism, and Freudianism. These rather materialistic approaches to life viewed conflict as the driving force behind progress. All relationships were reducible to the elements of biology, economics, or sex. Du Bois wrestled with the contradictions of this Eurocentric view, but unable to disengage himself, he recognized in his most centered Africanness that it never fully satisfied his spiritual yearning. Nevertheless, captured by the thought of human perfectibility through rationalism, he envisioned integration as the ultimate solution to America's racial issues.

Progress could be achieved if the legal conditions for such integration were encouraged. The creation of the National Association for the Advancement of Colored People (NAACP) helped to focus on the legal struggles of African-Americans. Du Bois' dream was to fight discrimination on demonstrative and legal grounds in the streets and in the courts. The integration of all social services and agencies were strongly agitated for in the South as well as in the North. The push for equality motivated Du Bois and became his motto. In every sector of American society he fought against discrimination and for integration, believing full integration to be the only hope for internal peace.

Despite his efforts, Du Bois became disillusioned; America lacked the moral character to fully integrate Africans into its democratic capitalist government system. But discrimination would only be eliminated with the most violent opposition because all government sectors operated negatively toward integration. A new consciousness eased itself into this great man as he became more Afrocentric, though he never fully sensed his nearness to victory.

Like Wallace Johnson and Nnamdi Azikiwe, Du Bois became more and more African in his outlook (Azikiwe, 1970). Transcending his American predicament through sheer intellectual courage, he lifted himself to a higher plane. He rejected the inherent racism in capitalism and pursued socialist thought. He moved toward the rejection of materialism which was deeply imbedded in Marxist thought. Because Du Bois was beyond the limitations of a Eurocentric analysis, he could never be restricted by Marxist thought.

He rallied against the small minds who categorized labor. He believed that his scholarly achievements constituted an indivisible part of work. In so doing, he acknowledged an African concept of the interconnectedness of all things.

Contemporary Marxists misunderstand the nature of racism, and contend that the only labor is manual labor, and therefore the only real worker is the manual laborer who creates economic value. Thus, I have been told by some misguided borthers that the inventor, theoretician, discoverer, and manager are not workers but economic parasites. Yet, from an Afrocentric perspective, manual labor functions as the value-creating prerequisite for the labor of thinkers and organizers. Whatever importance is attached to a strike by manual laborers must be seen in the light of objectives. Marxists believe that a manual laborers strike can stop any enterprise, and is therefore more important than other forms of labor. However, a rabbit caught in the proper machinery or birds in the right places can also shut down enterprises. We must aspire to more than shutting down; we must create, manufacture, and invent. Ours must be a world where we use all of our capabilities and our labor for the enhancement of people. Only in traditional western societies are there conflicts between classes; such is not the case when we operate from our traditional base of harmony. In the future, a committed Afrocentric viewpoint will be used to demonstrate the viability of harmony and the inoperative nature of conflict for true human advancement. Du Bois saw in our history the unfounding desire for unity, wholeness, and harmony (Du Bois, 1971).

Malcolm X

Malcolm X rejected the logic and practice of Eurocentric thought and became the standard bearer for the radical reversal of ideological dependence on white ideologies in the 1960's. He was, in their faces, its face, the single most terrifying sight to the forces of imperialism, capitalism, and racism. Like the indomitable Harriet Tubman in the nineteenth century, Malcolm X challenged the historical arrogance and political assertion of racial supremacy in America.

Despite the attempt by numerous revisionists to steal Malcolm's thunder, to reduce him to a sub-heading of Arabism, or a footnote in Marxism, he remains a Pan-African nationalist committed to the African cultural project. Even so, Malcolm understood the practical aspects of Africans living in an imperialist state, and he reacted to that condition with a keen analysis of the social and economic conditions of Africans in the United States.

He repeatedly acknowledged that Africans were persecuted because of their color not their religion. To the racist, it does not matter whether a black person is a Baptist, a Jew, a Muslim, or a Catholic; the racist only sees the color of a person's skin. Thus, on the basis of skin color alone, discrimination and persecution pursue the African person in the United States (Madhubuti, 1978).

Malcolm also used socialism as a way to sharpen his Pan-African nationalism. For example, he gave to us the full-blown analysis of the house and field slave that had occurred in Paul Robeson's discourse earlier. But in

Malcolm, this idea, a Rosesonian creation, became a much more concentrated attack on class divisions within the black community. Malcolm forcused on the ease of access to the white power structure and he defined class according to the level of identification with that structure (Stuckey, 1972). The so-called privileged position of the "house slave" occurred because such a slave had access to better food, to the master's ear, and to the master's favors. Now Malcolm understood that the house slave had no more control over the economic infrastructure than the field slave, in fact, the field slave could always take out anger by sabotaging the crops and machinery.

Malcolm's nationalism was severe because it called for the "house slave" to repudiate his or her own nature which had become the protection of the master's interests as his or her own interests. Most house slaves, because they would rather hurt themselves than their oppressors, found it difficult to act for their true interests. Fortunately, as Malcolm would often say, we didn't have too many house slaves. "The masses," he said, "were field slaves who worked hard and hated the oppressor."

Malcolm's vision stemmed not only from his personal experiences but also from his ideas. He knew what we know—that liberation could only come from a person's active will. We know that the oppressor refuses to admit guilt, to correct his evil ways, or to assist in the correction of corruption unless forced to do so by some means, economic, political, physical, or social. Malcolm's appeal to us was to use "any means necessary" to rid ourselves of the baggage of slavery and self-doubt.

In Malcolm's view, the United States owed African-Americans an enormous debt for the free labor rendered by our enslaved ancestors. The scandalous treatment of Africans existed, he said, because we had not stood up to demand our rights, totake our case to the World Court, to the United Nations. Malcolm, like Walter Rodney and Frantz Fanon, was a commentator, an activist commentator on the revolutionary road to an Afrocentric viewpoint.

Malcolm's multi-faceted views inspired Bobby Seale and Huey Newton, the black Marxist's, the Muslims, the Christians, and the systematic nationalist Maulana Karenga. In fact, the richness of Malcolm's philosophy generated a thousand ways to fight for liberation.

Karenga and Kawaida

Karenga understood that the time for redefinition passed in the 1960's and that the time for reconstruction had come. He had set out to tackle the most serious psychic problem facing Africans in America. Thus, while many African-Americans were busy marching, filing briefs, and trying to practice capitalism, Karenga was reconstructing African-American life and history.

Based upon the Nguzo Saba, the seven principles of nationhood which are umoja, kujichagulia, ujima, ujamaa, nia, kuumba, and imani, Karenga established a systematic ideology, *Kawaida* (Karenga, 1978). These pillars of faith are rooted in our traditions. Karenga relied deeply on history and tradition, and further enhanced our traditions by scientifically revealing the elements of a total ideology. A more perceptive thinker did not exist during the struggles of the 1960's. He possesses an original mind, freed of past restraints and opened to future possibilities. His strength exists in his cultural work which utilizes the seven criteria: history, mythology, creative motif, ethos, social organization, political organization, and economic organization. Karenga accurately understood the elements that were necessary to establish a system of thought.

Although his earlier concept of history was materialistic, he has emerged in the 1980's as a profound contributor to the Diopian school of Afrocentric thought. His books, *Introduction to Black Studies* and *The Husia*, advance the theoretical and humanistic African quest. Clearly he believes that an Afrocentric history must never separate the material and the spiritual. In the 1960's when Karenga chastised the Christian element for its "spookism," his purpose was instructive, but the result isolated the spiritual realities which are in fact parts of our history. Ancestors do in fact gather to inspire us and do bring us victory (Asante, 1978). We are people who appreciate the continuum of the spirit and matter; we do not distinguish between them. Indeed, our spirit, a personalism and humanism, animates matter as well as spirit. A renewed appreciation for this understanding makes Maulana one of the leading theoreticians of the twentieth century.

Mythology referred to a people's place in the universal scheme. Karenga correctly understood that we had to organize our mythology in order to give purpose, identity, and direction. All people have a mythology; Africans who have not given up their ethnic culture have their own mythologies that say how the world began and their place in it. African-Americans had not begun to systematize mythology until Elijah Muhammad and Maulana Karenga attempted to reconstruct our mythology. They both recognized the need for the creation of a systematic national history and mythology; yet Karenga's understanding led him in a direction which personified his individual political genius and collective cultural insistence. Karenga became a cultural scientist who emphasized the structural realities of culture. Therefore, Kawaida appeared to be typological as opposed to process. A student of the redefinition period, he learned from the works of

Garvey, Elijah, and Malcolm but it was Malcolm to whom Karenga could best relate. In Malcolm's staccato oratory, insistent eloquence, and international awareness of the African world, Karenga found optimism, insight, and creativity.

A creative motif, Karenga argued, was necessary for identity. How do we know what constitutes an Asian's Chineseness? What motifs reflect the Arab's Arabism? What distinguishing creative characteristics do we find for the Germans, the Spaniards? The African-American creative motif needed to be developed, according to Karenga. But our creative motif is within us; our energy needs tapping not developing. We contain within our souls the comprehensive potentialities of a powerful creative motif. Thus, we say that the creative motif of African-Americans can be discovered in our language, dress, behavior, and games. Many of these motifs are derived from our African heritage and appear in what we do with Adinkra, Adire goldweight designs, and hieroglyphics. Others are taken ferom our early institutions in America; and still others are created on the basis of our own essential Africanness (Karenga, 1978).

Ethos is the collective personality of the people. What do we convey to others when they think of us, see us, or hear us? Is our ethos musical? Karenga uses the concept of ethos to outline the most salient characteristics of a people's life. He was precise in his reference about our people, loving us in his philosophical genius, and hoping to force us to reconsider our *ethos*. He believed that a people can change the ethos by which they are known through collective will and consciousness. The Afrocentric response to ethos determines what is in the best interest of African people at a given time, and then creates, nationalizes, and justifies those symbols which validate our interests.

Karenga's work must be studied for its inherent consistency of thought and purpose. Although he is lyrical rather than narrative, analytical rather than prosaic, the sum total of his work represents Afrocentric genius. *Kawaida*, the philosophy expounded by Maulana, is, in effect, the most extensive development of a cultural ideology to grow out ofthe 1960's. Neither King nor Malcolm articulated the designs and details of a system of cultural reconstruction comparable to Karenga; Njia builds upon that foundation in its social and cultural work.

Njia: The Way

Njia is the collective expression of the Afrocentric worldview which is grounded in the historical experience of African people. It was predictable and inexorable. The stage was being set for Njia for over 100 years. Each level of awareness predictably led to the manifestation of Njia. Njia represents the inspired Afrocentric spirit found in the traditions of African-Americans, and the spiritual survival of an African essence in America. Thus, Njia places Afrocentricity in the African population of the Kiaspora and the continent. What occurred in the 1960's heightened the expectation and deepened the determination of our people to see Njia manifest. With its coming, we have a dynamic and flexible ideology rooted in the historical and cultural processes of African-Americans which is grounded simultaneously in the symbol and spirit of Africa. When we use Njia for our lives, we become essentially ruled by our own values and principles. Dispensing with alien views allows us to place Njia at our own center.

Njia is not the product of one or two minds; but the cumulative experiences of African people, expressed concretely in the lives of a small segment. It is found among African-Americans but also exists in several African countries. Njia becomes the main source of meditative activities and spiritual growth. When Njia is accepted, all things seem new, old things no longer please or seem adequate. The view of life, of the world, and of one's self is permanently altered. Acceptance of Njia is an acceptance of yourself. There is no way more perfect than the way derived from your own historical experiences; everything modern can be based upon our ancient foundations. Njia establishes a link to our fundamental, primordial truths.

A practice of Njia with the *Teachings of Njia* constitutes the beginning of reconstruction. People who come to Njia have usually passed through a redefinition phase. Njia bases reconstruction on Afrocentricity which becomes sacred to its teachings. Njia is both the name of the book and the name of the gathering. When you meet in Njia, you must meet around the *Teachings of Njia*. Njia meets on Sundays to renew strength but meetings may be held any and all time. There are six parts to an Njia meeting which are designed to incorporate the spirit into a functional aspect of life. These are: (1) Libation to Ancestors, (2) Poetry and Music Creativity and Expression, (3) Nommo: Generative Word Power, (4) Affirmation, (5) Teaching from Njia, and (6) Libation to Posterity. This pattern has become permanently a part of Njia which does not vary.

The libation to the ancestors honors the righteous brothers and sisters who have gone before us. Their achievements we should never forget. For this reason, the libation is recited prior to all meetings of Njia. Water is placed in three vases, one for each color of the liberation flag: red, green, black. the libator who stands behind the vases begins:

Libator: We call upon our ancestors far and near, father of our fathers
Audience: Mother of our mothers

Libator: To render mercy
Audience: To bear witness
Libator: To the liberation and victory of our people
Audience: Forever!
Libator: It is done! (The libator pours water from the red vase into the black vase which should be in the middle position.)

Following the libation, poetry and music allow for any free expression of creativity. Participants may read from any Afrocentric literature, sing a song, play a drum, blow a saxophone, or teach others how to perform a particular art form. When no one has more creative expression, the *mwalimu,* teacher, or *msingi,* founder, or *malaika,* beautiful one, says "appreciating what has been said, let us share Nommo."

During Nommo Afrocentric discussions of all the problems of the world occur. Here creative solutions are proposed. For example, someone may say, "I want to relate to you how I overcame negative behavior in a classroom discussion on ancient civilizations. When the European quoted from Toynbee on the lack of ancient civilizations in Africa, I was able to recite from Diop, Williams, and Jackson. In the past because my knowledge was limited and my self-confidence weak, I would have allowed that incident to pass, but not since Njia." In another example, Nommo is also the place where facts are disseminated, such as, "Robin Hood is an old African celebration form Egypt once called *Hruben-Hud* which was Anglicized by the English." Other kinds of information—historical, cultural, and political—can be discussed in Nommo. After Nommo, Njia affirms our survival and the God-force in us. Indeed, during affirmation, Njia is read and the participants reaffirm their belief in victorious thought.

The teaching of Njia is a conscious elaboration of its ideological bases. It seeks to awaken our deepest sensitivities to each other and our victorious postures toward the world. Njia is provocative and instructive and its teaching corresponds to this spirit. Following the teaching libation to posterity, which is accompanied by a collection of money, is performed.

As with the first libation to the ancestors, the final libation is done by a libator who leads the audience. At the completion of this libation the water in the green vase is poured into the black vase. The libator begins:

Libator: We call upon the spirit of our children
Audience: And their children
Libator: To witness what we have done
Audience: And who we are
Libator: To learn strength from us
Audience: And truth from us

Libator: And be not afraid as we are not afraid
Audience: And to come forth for you have been counted
Libator: It is done!

With the completion of Libation to Posterity, the audience rises and each person raises his right hand into the air for harambees. Harambee means "pulling together" in Kiswahili. The mwalimu or a designee leads the audience in seven harambees after the Nguzo Saba. Fruits and juices brought by the members of Njia are shared during the informal fellowship.

The meeting place for Njia must be Afrocentric. If it is not, it must be made so by Njia. All things should be perfect. This is the only way for Njia. Meeting places should have earth tones if possible; they should be in the round if it can be arranged. Plan for the time when you will have an Afrocentric architect to design an Njia with all modalities from your own center. A round building with the libation table in the middle is the best.

Finally, Njia, in a truly Afrocentric manner, pays its homage to Karenga's Kawaida, Elijah's Islam, Garvey's Transmigration, and Blyden's Intellectualism. It furthers them by first starting with the African-American center and positioning all things from the point. Njia counts time, for example, from the beginning again which was 1619. Thus all dates are accounted for on the basis of what side of year one they are. A date could be A.B.A. or B.B.A., *After the Beginning Again* or *Before the Beginning Again*. 1617 is written 2 B.B.A. and 1621 is 2 A.B.A. Although we may use other dates, Njia affirms for us our own place in history. It is necessary for the Afrocentric person to practice Njia for creative perfection. Although it is complete in its conceptualization, it must be made complete in its application. Thus I have presented to the grounds of Njia and the mode for practice. Our perfected application will come only after a great many people have seen the clearest darkness.

Toward Collective Consciousness

Since the eighteenth century, our thinkers have sought our political and economic union (Walker, 1965). This has proved to be a false hope because the choosing of illusions has made us weary of the rhetoric of unity. It is not unity that we must seek but collective consciousness. In Afrocentricity, there is a remarkable surge of consciousness that transcends the current emphasis on unity; this is the next act in our drama. Consciousness is now closer than it has ever been. While our sails have always been set in the proper direction, various winds of political and cultural change have kept us away from the open channel.

The free Africans who formed the Colored Conventions in the nineteenth century were successful in bringing African leaders together but those meetings never approached the expectations of activists like David Walker and Henry Highland Garnet. They were pleasant enough affairs: one could meet other blacks who had something to say about emancipation and much to say against slavery but the idea of a universal African consciousness never materialized. Such consciousness, which is the awareness of our collective history and future, where it has occurred has always been with a deep commitment to Africa itself. Only now are we beginning to come to proper terms with Africa and that is the reason it is only now that collective consciousness is closer than ever.

During the whole nineteenth century and much of the present century, we knew little and wanted to know little about Africa. This was true of Africans on the continent and in the Diaspora. Of course, there were some incredible people who refused to rest until they had made their peace with Africa. So even from the eighteenth century when we named our organizations and churches "African this-or-the-other" there were some amazing personalities who, as an old Afro-American expression has it, "hoed with a short-handle." They had little information with which to work regarding African geography, history, tradition, and culture, yet they forged for themselves an acceptable level of consciousness. Paul Cuffee, doing his best to recall the Twi "Kofi" as a name; Edward Blyden, establishing the bounds of our philosophical thought; Martin Delaney off to Africa to bargain with kings and chiefs for territories for a colony; and later both Booker T. Washington and W.E.B. Du Bois holding conferences on Africa. In a real sense it is impossible to understand Marcus Garvey without his search for the essence of the African's soul which he promulgated to millions of people. So exceptional personalities, like Garvey and Bishop Turner, stood against the storm and kept the lights burning to point the way.

Consciousness precedes unity. I believe that this is what Malcolm X understood when he advanced Black National Consciousness to counter White National Consciousness. Malcolm X recognized that unity meant understanding that integration was an attempt to absorb black culture into white culture. What Malcolm X argued is that consciousness must be addressed by the masses. But we must appreciate the fact that acquisition of consciousness is part pedagogical and part phenomenological. We learn from our teachers who have studied our history and given attention to our traditions and revolutionary possibilities; and we learn from the lowest stages of conflict with a racist opposition whenever we assert ourselves. Our consciousness grows at each stage until we are finally clear in our Afrocentricity.

The particular nature of this consciousness expresses our shared commitments, fraternal reactions to assaults on our humanity, collective awareness of our destiny, and respect for our ancestors. When we come to acceptance, as surely we are coming, of this consciousness we will experience the rise of Afrocentricity. But consciousness is more than acceptance, it is response, it is action demonstrable and meaningful in terms of psychological and political actions. There are numerous consciousnesses and that black consciousness is a collective consciousness for us made singularly important by our unique presence in a predominantly white if not predominantly alien society. Our reaction to the forces surrounding us reflects our self-consciousness—our knowableness in relationship to other such selves who must determine how to respond to the selfsame social forces. To state this, is to speak directly, that is, and expose bluntly the crux of our previous *predicament* of consciousness. You see, we must respond to the external forces, there is no escaping that responsibility. Whether it is merely our presence in a crowded room, our essays in popular journals, or in verbal encounters, we are victims of response, imprisoned by the necessity to say what needs to be said, or be who we must, or write as we must in order to maintain and extend our sanity. There is not question that we shall keep our sanity, our proverbs will take care of that. But there is a serious question about the expansion of our sanity and by that I mean our consciousness. We shall have little trouble in the rise of the spirits expanding the consciousness of non-blacks, but we might suffer from over-extension, actually the eating away of own consciousness as we attempt to tell the truth elsewhere. Therefore, I say that extending our sanity is the *predicament* of our consciousness.

Certainly this *predicament* as I choose to call it is a significant moment of crisis, but still more significant is how we shall deal with it in the rise of the spirits. This is not merely a question of technique but also of existence in the most precise sense because it relates to our total reality and experience in this society. What we must guard against is the dismantling of our warning systems, the demise of sixth sense perceptions about human relations in a racist context, the lowering of defenses against cute racist fads, and the juggling of concepts and terminology which seek to re-enslave us. So our response to the threat of a *predicament* of consciousness must be constant vigilance and positive assertions to counteract the erosion of our consciousness. When Hollywood throws a "shuffle" on us and has small children, ten and twelve, talking about "I'm your pusher-man," it is time for us to do some serious questioning, not just of Hollywood writers, but of black actors and actresses who participate in such movies. I have never believed that we were so devoid of images of heroes or heroines that we had to resort to Hollywood for cultural guidance. And in many instances, the movie industry is competing with our thrust for consciousness; we become too easy victims of what is projected. Fortunately, we are dealing with self first. The initial lessons are hard; the rest are comparatively easy. Once we have entertained the ideas of consciousness, mulled them over, accepted the concept of Pan-Africanism, related our Afrocentricity to Africa and the Diaspora, and made terms with our ancestors, we will have dealt successfully with the *predicament* of consciousness.

All of this suggests a personalism, an awareness and an acceptance individually, before we can discuss collectivism in the matter of consciousness. It is the total individual acceptances that constitute the collective consciousness. Thus it becomes necessary for African-Americans to come to terms with slave names. To come to terms does not mean to acquiesce in what has been done historically, but to challenge and modify the mistakes of the past. We are victims of our names because we have previously refused to assert that we are African people. It used to be fashionable for blacks to say that they were only part African because of their Indian, Irish, Jewish, Chinese, or Gypsy blood. For some reason these blacks never admitted having English blood, the most likely foreign strain present in African-Americans. Nonetheless, our genes, as those of most peoples, have been mingled with those of various other ethnic groups. This combination itself has produced a new people, springing from the carpet of a peculiar psycho-social experience. But while this is so, it is also a fact that the core of our collective being is African, that is, our awareness of separateness from the Anglo-American experience is a function of our historical memory, the memory we have frequently denied or distorted. Such experiences are rooted in our ancestral home and defined by social and legal sanctions of four hundred years in America. Regardless to our various complexions and degrees of consciousness we are by virtue of commitments, history, and convictions an African people. Afrocentricity, therefore, is only superficially related to color, it is more accurately a philosophical outlook determined by history.

During the 1960's and 1970's we came to terms with our collective name and chose to be either "African," "Afro-American," or "black" rather than "Negro" or "colored." We must certainly sooner or later make the same observation on a personal level that we have made on a collective level. In the future there is no question that this will be undertaken on many occasions. It is not only logical, it is practical and we have always responded to logic and pragmatism. The practical value of changing our names is an identification of names with people. We are an African people and it is logical for us to possess African names. Already we are on the verge of a breakthrough, young black parents are seeking African names for their children in an attempt to assign meaning to their identity.

Most African-American names are remnants of the plantation masters' names, some seldom seen among contemporary whites, for example, Washington, Jefferson, Lincoln, Bennett, Jackson, and others. After emancipation the majority of Africans who had been known by only one name on the plantation or farm had to select second or last names for legal and social purposes. There were no longer simply "Moses," "Jemima," "Remus," and "Plenty" who belong to Mr. So-and-So. Having little knowledge, and lacking information about Africa, the freedmen chose names that they had heard among the whites, and occasionally, the names of their previous masters. In some cases, our ancestors selected names of the most famous white Americans, thus the preponderance of Washington, Lincoln, Adams, Jefferson, and Jackson. Although free blacks in the North often retained the slave names they had prior to manumission, several attempted to acquire what they thought were African names. They obviously rebelled against being captives of white names. Defined collectively by whites as "Negroes" and identified individually by white names, they were bodies without spirits, people without dignity, whether they knew it or not. You cannot be circumscribed by someone else, and at the same time have a healthy respect for yourself as a person. The essence of psychological health is that one deals and is capable of dealing with his identity. It is impossible to come to terms with consciousness unless we learn this lesson first. What changes with the changing of our names is how we perceive ourselves and how others perceive us. Changing of names will not in itself change economic and social oppression; but it will contribute to the creation of new economic, political, and social forces that anticipate substantive change. The name changing action is at once a rejection and an acceptance, a necessary condition for a new perspective on our place in the world. There is little question that how we perceive ourselves influences how others perceive us. This being so, and other things being equal, the acceptance of African names will establish a more distinct perception of our Afrocentricity. A Muslim takes an Arabic name; a Christian takes a Christian name; we take African names.

For some blacks the name change will be traumatic; for some whites our rejection of white names will be dramatic. Having sought to become "white" even to the extent of maintaining our slave names which identified us with the white master, we still find it difficult to discard the trappings of slavery. We become our own worst enemies while we remain tied to white cultural, historical, and symbolic systems. So exchanging Eurocentric names for Afrocentric names will be traumatic for some blacks; some will even refuse to do it. On the other hand whites who have grown accustomed to our "white" names will see the exchange of names as a dramatic indication of our desire for an identity separate from that of whites. Quite apart from anything else many whites have been as much influenced by the total distortion and misrepresentation of Africa as blacks have been. So it is relatively easy to find whites who do not see African-Americans as Africans. This incredible insanity was put on display in several southern cities a few years ago when an African-American wearing a Yoruba agbada and calling himself Chief Olaitan Olayide was greeted with honor in places in the South where James L. Smith would not have been able to enter. Dressed in a "Botany 500" and calling himself James L. Smith or even Dr. James L. Smith the same African-American would have been refused service. My case is that whites have never had to react to us as a people with a history apart from slave history. Indeed we have seldom confronted that history ourselves; that is why I contend that the acceptance of the past will be the beginning of our liberation. Dignity is not bestowed, and it cannot be taken, it can and must be accepted. But the acceptance is a matter of consciousness and consciousness is the result of experience and conviction. The experience we have already had; the conviction comes when we can act on the basis of our history.

There is another facet to this whole question of exchanging names, namely, what names shall we Africans take? It is sometimes suggested by pundits, blacks as well as whites, that we seldom know our original African name. Such suggestion, of course, is an indication of the trauma, the fear of blacks assuming an African identity. Almost any traditional African name is more appropriate for us than say an English, German, or Irish name. Can you imagine a white European with a name like *Kofi Adegbola*? Or a Japanese in the United States, Brazil, or Japan with a name like *Gerhard Casmir*? Coming to terms with consciousness means accepting an African name because only such a name reflects our consciousness. Of course, for those blacks who see their history only from the time of slavery and from a European perspective the retention of slave names may be more psychologically comfortable. Furthermore, assuming an African name is simply a renunciation of white personal identity symbols. There is something very wrong with one's understanding of the multi-racial character of the United States when one believes that the rejection of white values is a rejection of the United States. Be that as the ancestors will have it, we must decide whether we will assume names more reflective of our core identity or not.

I see the choosing of an African name as participatory, inasmuch as it contributes to the total rise to consciousness, which, ultimately, is what the rise of the African spirit is all about. There can be no effective discussion of a united front, a joint action, a community of interest until we come to good terms with collective consciousness, the elementary doctrine of economic, political, and social action. The choice of a name is only one small step in a large process, but it is a beginning, an understanding and a return. Quite certainly those of us who maintain the superficial materials of European cultural styles will have to rethink our blonde wigs, our fried, dyed, and swept to the side hairstyles, and cocaine-on-the-brain mentality.

Suppose you met a European whose name was Osei Owusu who dressed in Kente cloth, and danced the Kete or Adua, what would you think if he told you that he did not like Africans or Africa? When you give yourself a European name, dress like the European, behave toward others as the European often has done, who is to say you are not European in mind no matter how hard you protest. Reflect on the truth and you shall see a mighty light.

Chapter 2
The Constituents of Power

Language Liberation

An ideology for liberation must find its existence in ourselves, it cannot be external to us, and it cannot be imposed by those other than ourselves; it must be derived from our particular historical and cultural experience. Our liberation from the captivity of racist language is the first order of the intellectual. *There can be no freedom until there is a freedom of the mind.* As Lorenzo Turner understood, language is essentially the control of thought. It becomes impossible for us to direct our future until we control our language. The sense of language is in precision of vocabulary and structure for a particular social context. If we allow others to box us into their concepts, then we will always talk and act like them. Black language must possess instrumentality, that is, it must be able to do something for our liberation; such a position is not foreign to our particular or collective international struggle. Liberation is fundamentally a seizure of the instruments of control. If the language is not functional, then it should have no place in our vocabulary. In every revolution, the people have first seized the instruments of idea formation and then property production.

History is instructive for us. In the thirteen American colonies, the rebels took *liberty* and *parliamentary representation* and gave them definitions foreign to the ruling classes. In 1789, in the French Revolution, the so-called first modern revolution, the people took *liberté, égalité,* and *fraternité* and made them instruments for a collective will to power. The Soviet Union's revolution of 1917 could not have succeeded without the creative eloquence of Trotsky and Lenin. They understood that to free the masses from abject slavery it was necessary to teach them to think in different terms. In Algeria, in Cuba, in Mozambique, in Zimbabwe, and in Angola the same pattern appears. We cannot seek only to be opposites of the oppressor, that simply makes us "reactionaries," and "reactionaries" are conservative not progressive. The aim of systematic nationalism is to make the language ours, to claim a new language, not merely an opposite language.

Africans have shown a remarkable ability to humanize any language we have spoken whether it was Portuguese, English, Spanish, French, or Russian. What Nicolas Guillen did to Spanish, what Alexander Pushkin did to Russian, what Langston Hughes did to English, and what Aime Cesaire, the greatest of all poets, did to French, suggest that it is in the soul of our people to seize and redirect language toward liberating ideas and thought.

African-Americans are an historic people. We have met the challenges of an alien culture, a racist mentality, and an exploitative enterprise with our African ability to transform reality with words and actions. We must nourish this capability. Maulana Karenga argues that "no people can turn its history and humanity over to alien hands and expect social justice and respect" (Karenga, 1979). Language is the essential instrument of social cohesion. Social cohesion is the fundamental element of liberation.

All language is epistemic. Our language provides our understanding of our reality. *A revolutionary language must not befuddle; it cannot be allowed to confuse.* Critics must actively pursue the clarification of public language when they believe it is designed to whiten the issues. We know through science and rhetoric; they are parallel systems of epistemology. Rhetoric is art and art is as much a way of knowing as science.

When the oppressor seeks to use language for the manipulation of our reality; Nommo, for ourselves, and of ourselves, must continue the correct path of critical analysis. Such a path is not dictated necessarily by the oppressor's rhetoric but *Njia* for the Afro-American intellectual. Objectivism, born of the history, culture, and materials of our existence must be at the base of our talk and our essaying.

It is necessary to understand the power of this concept. Some of our poets and preachers have understood it. We must gather the materials and sources from ourselves first. We must then move to enlarge upon our precepts and concepts by constant clarification and progressivism. The language of the exploiter is vile, corrupt, and vulgar. For him racism is non-existent because it is now merely discrimination or pragmatically the inequality of opportunity. We cannot permit this easy slide into exploitative rhetoric. *There is no such thing as a black racism against whites; racism is based on fantasy; black views of whites are based on fact.* Racist language makes the victim the criminal. We must repudiate that thinking.

The use of the terms *ethnicity, disadvantaged, minority,* and *ghetto* are antithetical to our political consciousness which is indivisible from the international political struggle against racism. Our American situation has never been defined as "ethnic" until now when it is beneficial for the oppressor. This is new and must be understood. Our situation has been one where racism victimizes Africans as a race. Racism is the fundamental contradiction in African-American existence. It is also the case in Brazil, South Africa, and Namibia. It is too early for us to allow that to be forgotten. But this twist in talk is due to the fact that race functions as a fundamental category of class in the United States. The ruling classes in America have moved to interpret European ethnics as similar to blacks in their predicament. Such rhetoric generates class conflict which hides racism, the primary reality of American society. Class conflict does exist, yet such conflict is also manipulated by language in a society where rulers are isolated from the ruled. Language serves as an instrument of social restraint. There are certain things you do not say to some people and surely some things you do not do to them. Our breaking away from the structures of the oppressor's language will be instructive at a class as well as at the race level.

Those among us who have been trapped into using Marxist language have understood neither our history nor that of Marxism. While it is possible for socialism to find expression in places outside of its original intellectual context, no context is ever the same. Each context invites a variation in the doctrine; and some contexts may find the expression of the doctrine unnatural. Needless to say, it cannot and has not been imposed on those contexts which would have responded more naturally to other political expressions. Mozambique is not Cuba is not China and so forth. An adaptive process takes precedence over the presence of the doctrine. This is true of capitalism as well. But those among us who become dogmatic in any doctrine except on founded upon principles and assumption derived from our historical context will always make the wrong analysis. You cannot use the language of socialism only and expect to escape ambiguity.

Systematic nationalism does not negate socialism (Asante, 1978). Socialism provides us with some possibilities of freedom from class exploitation but our political liberation must come primarily from notions forged from our social experiences. Our language must reflect liberation as well. We have been exploited, discriminated, oppressed, humiliated, and assassinated. Our political doctrines must speak to that reality. Since language is the instrument for conveying that truth, our language must be aggressive, and innovative. As inventive people, we must make sure that our linguistic inventions are functional in a socially and politically cohesive way. This means we must rid our language of degrading terms which have been inherited from our oppressor.

Our history is replete with political cycles as evidenced by the historical discontinuity of our struggle. The basic political quality, exemplified in our perpetual will to freedom frequently has been diverted by subversion, discontinuous explications, and personality phenomena into rarefied and stratified discussions which have little basis in experience, the most radical of empiricisms. Systematic nationalism has occupied and will continue to reign supreme in our ideological confrontation with racist language and behavior because of its groundedness in the folk beliefs of our people, its historical locus in creative struggle, and the power of the rhetoric which it commands. Social and political conquest are the results of intellectual and spiritual conquest, and time does not change the fact.

The complexity of our intellectual heritage defies brief recapitulation. Yet when we contemplate the politics of communication and continual restructuring of black language to accommodate the intensification of struggle we must remember the contributions of Damas, Blyden, Padmore, Locke, W.E.B. Du Bois, Malcolm X, C.L.R. James. We are the inheritors of a noble tradition. Add to this tradition the wealth of values passed from generation to generation, and we have a formidable cultural inheritance as well.

However, we cannot peddle good feelings. We must judge relevance, evaluate the historical realism, and apply appropriate models for liberation. I seek a language whose axiological basis resides in history but those pragmatic manifestations are in our present reality. History is self compliments; the present puts us face to face with ourselves as we are. Our history cannot be left for others to write but neither should our present be turned over to others. All oppressor nations attempt to create taboos or legal prohibitions to block languages which might change the way people think. Such oppressor societies try to perpetuate their own politics by blocking competing language forms.

Lessons from History

The Third Reich created the *Regenspropagandaministerium*. Information ministries frequently have been turned to suppressive uses. In the United States we must combat a huge bureaucracy which has a life of its own. Pronouncements, memoranda, and policies are generated by the internal energy of the system so that an individual working in the bureau becomes merely an informational link in the process already begun. There seems to be no beginning or ending. *The force of our truth must be so deafening that even the bureaucrats will have to change their language to accommodate the reality.* This was being accomplished during the 1960's and 1970's. What happened of course was that the media stole the irony and facilitated acceptance of "right on" with a bic ballpen advertisement "write on." Lyndon Johnson was to "overcome" and "Black is beautiful, so is green" became Reverend Ike parody. The white Left wanted all power to the people, and so did the white Right. Black power alone seemed to have escaped this whitening process, but even here we had Nixonians rushing to explain that it meant black capitalism.

The vicious South African supremacist state has stolen liberating language through the manipulation of the communication process. They have employed two methods of control: (1) the modification of the meaning of words and (2) the suppression of opposition language. Consequently, the people battle against distortions, fallacies, and lies, as well as physical oppression. However, the people will win because the spirit of resistance to evil is ultimately more creative than the evil will to destroy.

The language of personal racism expressed in *de facto*, and *de jure* situations was called institutional racism by Stokely Carmichael and Charles Hamilton. Their creative exposition, based upon the people's historical objections, and mass action campaigns, produced institutional changes. The government mandated affirmative action programs and it seemed as if institutional racism was being legislated out of existence. The talk went right along with the legislation. Those of us who had marched, been jailed and clubbed thought that progress was being made. But only the rhetoric of oppression has changed. Personal racism remains unabated. What happened was that *institutional racism* gave way to *process racism*.

Process racism as a metamorphosis of institutional racism dominates the society. Jimmy Carter's Georgia church dispensed with an institutional stand against blacks and adopted a process stand by setting up a screening committee. The idea is to give the impression of running while standing still. Our aggressive language must attack, not institutional or process racism but personal racism. Scholars must study the psyches of racists, their lifestyles and the value-beliefs systems in order to devise language strategies to deal with reactionary postures.

Our task is *elephant*. The massiveness of it can be met by skillful rhetoricians understanding the immensity of the problem. A mobilizing language would elevate nationalism above religious sects, sex roles, and social class distinctions. As nationalism counteracted ethnic divisions and social class in Mozambique and Zimbabwe it can also do in African America. Everyone from merchant to laborer, from Christian to Muslim, from intellectual to illiterate, and from aspiring socialist to aspiring capitalist must be mobilized by a new language of consciousness. Malcolm X acknowledged this when he said we were attacked because of our blackness and not because we were Baptist, Methodist, or Muslim. Religious and class struggles must be subordinated to national struggle in an aggressive stance toward racism. Such substantive rhetoric, even acted out in the formation of group cohesion, cannot eliminate all internal contradictions. What is necessary, however, is that the national cause becomes the principal interest of the people and all other interests become subordinate considerations.

In the resurgence of nationalism, which is an arm of pan-Africanism, we cannot permit the hijacking of the movement by those who understand neither our history nor our struggle. Our last cycle was a lesson in history. Strident rhetoric between different political organizations professing the liberation of the people gave aid and comfort to the enemy forces. Despite the rhetoric it is clear now that the Black Panthers foreshadowed the decline of nationalism in the late sixties. Streetwise brothers and sisters learned the proper tenets of Marx and Mao but failed to study David Walker, Henry Garnet, Marcus Garvey, Kwame Nkrumah and Malcolm X. Bobby Seale, co-founder of the Panthers, often found himself trying to moderate the rhetoric of Mao's four works and other teachings. Thus, a brilliant community program which inspired thousands was stagnated because it lacked an historical perspective. Seale recognized this more than Huey Newton and sought to elevate the consciousness of radical black history. Nonetheless, their rhetoric remained without the historical content so necessary for a correct interpretation of our American experience.

Afrocentric writers restructure the language to tell the truth. Our logicians and rhetoricians must not let us fall into any linguistic chasms. The major human rights problem in the world today in terms of extent of exploitation, class suffering, and racial oppression is in southern Africa. We cannot allow ourselves to be beguiled by any rhetoric which elevates the suffering of Russian Jews any higher than the plight of Africans in Azania. It is our task to *endarken* the people that national struggle Azania is a part of our struggle. We must demonstrate that those who minimize the suffering in Azania are blinded by racism, and to the fact that Mandela is a victim of white racism. Thousands suffer with him in South African jails. Let us build a language of truth. Upon the base of this language can be erected the pyramids of progressive national liberation.

The communication of our national will to liberty through adequate actions and symbols is the single most important fact in cultural liberation. Whether in the use of language or other symbols the propagation of culture views and senses distinguishes one society from another. The cardinality of productive forces, technologically derived modes of dissemination, pre-empts all other concerns with the nature of our political rhetoric. The control of mass media technology, electronic and print, by reactionary forces around the world must be neutralized by the persistence of our historically and culturally derived mechanism of political propagation. We must create, innovate, and bombard the communication channels with positive images, which will constitute a revolutionary response to racist repression. In voice, percussion, writing, and images we should express the totality of our American experience, knowing both its separateness from and its connectedness to a Pan-African world. Certain distinctions, to be sure, exist within societies because of the *emphasis* placed on the productive forces and the political objectives. The imperialism of rhetoric, couched in either capitalist or socialist terms, must be curbed by an aggressive language which finds it *fons et origo* in our natural will to freedom. A language, dedicated to such an end, regularly expanded with relevant ideas and symbols, is crucial to our liberation from racist concepts. So when you greet one another say, "Peace, freedom belongs to you."

Types of Intelligence

Three types of intelligence exist in the world: *creative intelligence, recreative intelligence,* and *consumer intelligence.* The most valuable type of intelligence is that which communicates with the whole earth by remaining open to associations, ideas, spaces, and possibilities. Disciplined attitudes rooted in Afrocentric images and symbols can create endless combinations; there are numerous examples from our history of the constructive potential of creative combinations.

Re-creative intellectuals are able to take the vision of the creative intellectuals to new heights. They do this by constantly seizing upon ideas and propagating them with great clarity. Thus Malcolm X was the reproductive mind for the work of Elijah Muhammad; Halisi and Baraka propagated the works of Karenga; Lenin and Mao expounded the principles of Marx; Jesus had twelve initial teachers; Muhammad sent Abu Bakr and others to the various parts of the world; King had his Abernathy and Jackson. These reproductive minds may be creative in other areas but in the situations mentioned they were recreative. Some of the greatest people known in the history of the world are reproductive minds. In Afrocentricity there will be numerous poets, scholars, teachers, artists, and philosophers who will surpass those who laid the foundation in terms of propagation.

The third type of intelligence is that of the practical intellectual who neither creates nor recreates but rather consumes and utilizes ideas. In an Afrocentric society, all intelligence is accepted as containing the God-force. Yet it is understood that not everyone can appropriate its power for every purpose. Some people are actualizing and recreative, and still others are actively practicing and consuming. There is nothing inherently wrong with consumption; one must know what is being consumed.

With this analysis of intelligence it becomes possible for us to see the connectedness of intelligence to nature and culture. The Afrocentric perspective envisions one wholistic, organic process. Thus, all political, artistic, economic, ethical, and aesthetic issues are connected to the context of Afrocentric knowledge. Everything that you do; all that you are and will become is intricately wrapped with the Kente of culture. Mind and matter, spirit and fact, truth and opinion, are all aspects or dimensions of one vital process.

There can be no good intelligence except as it is reflected in the nature of things. All propositions, statements about good, truth, falsehood and evil, rest with the Afrocentric concept of nature. What is the nature of things? For us, naturalism in of itself is inert and does not explain our spirituality, or vitality, our creative and dynamic energy. Idealism begins with too much abstractness to account for process; static concepts box in our vital nature as a people.

All things are possible as actions; all objects are integral to nature as objects; and all phenomena are potentially good or evil according to their cultural use. Afrocentricity views all things as integrated with culture and nature. We are one. Facts, then, are not intelligence or knowledge about things. The knowledge of a thing can only come through an act of judgment involving concept and ideology. What concept do you posses and in what ideological framework is it contained? These questions speak to the direction, intensity, purpose, and identity of the seeker. Reality exists not merely as a reality of facts but a reality of creation and perception.

Intellectual Vigilance

Afrocentricity maintains intellectual vigilance as the proper posture toward all scholarship which ignores the origin of civilization in the highlands of East Africa. Our need is to advance the theory of Afrocentricity through critical attention to what is written and spoken by those who profess knowledge regardless to their ancestry. Arnold Toynbee, for example, wrote that whites founded four ancient civilizations while blacks found none. This is not merely Eurocentricity; it is malicious racism of the type we have confronted and exposed for the last two hundred years. We know because of our Afrocentric consciousness that only one ancient civilization could be considered European in origin, Greece. And Greece itself is a product of its interaction with African civilizations. Among ancient civilizations Africans gave the world, Ethiopia, Nubia, Egypt, Cush, Axum, Ghana, Mali, and Songhay. These ancient civilizations are responsible for medicine, science, the concept of monarchies and divine-kingships, and an Almighty God. Afrocentricity establishes a profound movement in critical reading as well as critical thinking. To the degree that we begin to examine the literary perspectives of black and white writers we will understand the power of symbols.

Our collective consciousness must question writers who use symbols and objects which do not contribute meaningfully to our victory. How could a black writer be allowed to use symbols which contradict our existence and we not raise our voices? Afrocentric criticism must hold especially accountable the works of African, continental or diasporan. We have failed to be critical of the Alvin Aileys and Arthur Mitchells in dance for example because we felt that we should not criticize blacks who are creative. The times are surely different and we must now open the floodgates of protest against any non-Afrocentric stances taken by writers, authors, and other intellectuals or artists. Afrocentricity sustains our lives through self affirmation.

The Provable Bases

Afrocentricity reorganizes our frame of reference so that we become the center of analysis and synthesis. As such, it becomes the source of regeneration of our values and beliefs. Indeed, this movement recaptures the collective will responsible for ancient Egypt and Nubia. The past, however, only tells us what is possible; it cannot fight for us except in a psychological sense. We accept the psychological support and laud ourselves for having ancestors who gave us such a powerful legacy. How can Hansel and Gretel or Jack and Jill continue to be the names, with all that those names imply, of our children's clubs? What insidious animal eats away at our brains and causes us to sleep when our own children are being stolen away from us? What is a child to believe when he or she grows up? Is it to be that we were so preoccupied with a whiteness that we could not reinforce our own heritage for them, even if only in names of our clubs? Understand gently, what we choose to call ourselves and our organizations reflects on our own consciousness. Every act must be deliberately chosen for its historic purpose and mission. Nothing that is done can ever be glossed over again; it must be considered in terms of its implications for the future. Our time is now.

The breakdown of our central political organizations from the disintegration of Egypt during the coming of the foreigners all the way to the enslavement of Africans represents one massive slide away from our center. Since the colonial era, many countries have adopted all of the symbols and behaviors of decadent Western societies. Thus, in the Diaspora and on the continent we become victims of Eurocentric behaviors. Instead of modeling governments on the traditional values and patterns of our people, we follow systems which have proved themselves neither in their native lands nor among us. And those structures which have existed for thousands of years are often abandoned in favor of an imported ideology. Because of this lack of consciousness the people will demand a return to the basic principles which have always placed us at the center. Afrocentricity does not champion reactionary postures and it is not regresssive. Nevertheless Afrocentricity seeks to modify even African traditions where necessary to meet the demands of modern society. A halt is called to the disintegration of our collective consciousness by introducing Afrocentricity at every step. This is necessary to shock the unconsciousness into awakening postures.

Some of us have been asleep so long and so deeply that we were not able to heed the words of Cheikh Anta Diop and Chancellor Williams (Diop, 1974, 1978; Williams, 1974). But when the *New York Times* came out with the story that Nubia had an older civilization than Egypt it validated the Afrocentric histories of Diop, Ben-Jochannan, and Williams in the minds of even the most stubborn Eurocentric Africans (Ben-Jochannan, 1972). Numerous writers have challenged the basic premises of Afrocentricity by expounding a Eurocentric viewpoint of everything from culture to the origin of civilization. The African writers who have mimicked such Eurocentric formulas are unable to think in an Afrocentric frame of mind. As a result, they relinquish their thoughts and research to Eurocentric purposes, and consequently deny their own humanity. Enslavement of the mind is the most pernicious kind of enslavement because the person so enslaved will never be able to see clearly for himself. Breaking the mental chains only occurs when a person learns to take two sets of notes on almost everything encountered in the Western world. If they say that Shakespeare is the greatest writer, know Cesaire, Du Bois, Hughes, Soyinka, Guillen, Ngugu, Pushkin. If they say that ballet is classical dance, know that it is no more classical than Adowa or a Mfundalai Shairi Dansi. If they say Bach is universal, know that Bach cannot be anymore universal than John Coltrane or Duke Ellington. After one has established a sound basis for knowledge, other truths will find their way. In this manner the frames of reference change and become liberatory for us, expanding our horizons to ourselves.

The brother who thought he was getting over, meaning, showing how white he had become replied to the student that he was really a writer who just happened to be black. There is no such animal as that. One is always born with a certain heritage and identity; to deny it is to deny yourself. Garth Fagan of The Bucket Dance Company made such an antihuman statement when asked about being a black choreographer. Although his inspiration is most definitely African he copped out and told the New York *Voice* (June, 1987) that "he happened to be black." The reaction of most people was "I guess you did!" A symbol revolution based upon Afrocentricity is necessary for the salvation of our sanity as a people.

When a writer seeks to write about life, death, birth, love, happiness, or sadness, the first thing that should come to mind is himself, his people, and their motifs. If he writes about his own people, he is writing about a universal experience of people. Do not be captured by a sense of universality given to you by the Eurocentric viewpoint; such a viewpoint is contradictory to your own ultimate reality. Isolate, define, and promote those values, symbols, and experiences which affirm you. Only through this type of affirmation can we really and truly find our renewal; this is why I speak of it as a reconstruction instead of a redefinition. Actually what we have to do is not difficult because the guidelines are clearly established in our past. We must continue to be *excellent, provocative, organized, educated,* and *dependable.* Understand something, these qualities represent our natural state. We are already practicing the attributes; now we must perfect them in ourselves and others.

Afrocenticity does not condone inefficiency in its name. Our history gives us enough examples to demonstrate this point. Those who have truly acted from their own Afrocentric centers have always had admirable records of excellence and efficiency. Consider the work of David Walker who was so inspired by the convention held in Boston that the next year, 1828, he began to write and have broadcast his dynamic pamphlet, *An Appeal to the Colored Citizens of the World.* Walker did it because he loved himself, and consequently he loved the people whose son he was. What he did was profound in its power and excellence. It took courage, commitment, and time. David Walker's victory was achieved in the face of nearly overwhelming odds for a freedom fighter in his time. He planned, strategized, and succeeded in having copies of his powerful pamphlet distributed as far south as Georgia. Every victory over fascism, apartheid, and racism has been won by rational fanatics who have shown their commitment to excellence. You must develop the will to see a project through to conclusion. Don't start a class and then stop it because you did not think it through; and don't request information and then refuse to pick it up and use it. These are all typical anti-Afrocentric behaviors. They do not reflect yourself at the center. You are always the center of what you do.

The chain of reasoning that leads to the denunciation of racism starts with your ultimate reality which is blackness. Indeed the racist must be allowed to act; he cannot act unchecked unless we allow him to act. Thus, when you have any hint of racism occurring in your presence, confront it immediately and directly. Be sure of your ground, then attack the racist with convincing arguments. You can always be sure of your ground if you have a clear conception of who you are and what you will and will not allow to be said or done to others like yourself. I used Afrocentricity as a reference point and spoke up firmly and directly. The matter was resolved.

We need not act belligerently in cases where we put our center to work for us. Our facts act for us. Langston Hughes was more universal than Robert Frost; and he had a more pleasant and humanistic personality, too. With this fact I do not have to beat someone over the head; I simply state my truth. That is the way to practice Afrocentricity. There is little need to make grand stands on issues. Our facts are in our history, use them. Their facts are in their history, and they have certainly used theirs. Denounce racism by the strength of moral and political will. Our collective will secures the victory that we reach with our historical and cultural facts. Allow Shango, Obatala, Simple, Legba, Chaka, Nzingha, Candace, Oduduwa, and Menes to announce your superior knowledge. When you sit in classes and listen to lecturers speak of Keats, Yeats, Twain, Wordsworth, Frost, Eliot, and Goethe, you had better be able to call upon Baraka, Shange, Welsh, Guillen, Cesaire, Abiola, Ngugi, and Okai. Not to call upon these spirit voices when you are bombarded with alien shadows makes you a victim of the most detestable isolation and alienation from your own past and present.

In a revolutionary context, the force which secures the strongest commitment to Afrocentricity will always occupy the central position of power. This is true for political parties among us that are engaged in warfare against white minority regimes. When the core is clear, other things become clear. Peripheral concepts will hover around the fringes of power but the real core must be Afrocentric for effectiveness. The more we shave off the fringes, the more pronounced and sufficient our Afrocentricity. Pure Afrocentricity is a compelling force (Welsh, 1978). Yet we are naturally propelled toward it by our unyielding humanism. Express symbols to the survival of human spirit in the midst of materialism, we are positive motion. In art, science, medicine, engineering, and literature we are the vanguards for humanism and sensitivity.

Afrocentricity can stand its ground among any ideology or religion: Marxism, Islam, Christianity, Buddhism, or Judaism. Your Afrocentricity will emerge in the presence of these other ideologies because it is from you. It is a truth, even though it may not be their truth. This singularity of purpose is close to Afrocentricity because it does not ignore logic and emotion. They are inseparable in this context and most Africans no matter how distorted their realities will accept the cultural basis of Afrocentricity. It is like a fish swimming in water, it cannot escape the water. Its choice is whether to swim or not, that is, to activate. There is nothing the fish can do about the existence of the water. This is why the contemporary philosopher Karenga says "Our Africanity is our ultimate reality." As a people, our most cherished and valuable achievements are the achievements of spirit. With an Afrocentric spirit, all things can be made to happen, it is the source of genuine revolutionary commitment.

Chapter 3
Analysis and Science

Criticism and Analysis

A new criticism emerges to support Afrocentricity which introduces relevant values; denounces non-Afrocentric behavior; and promotes analysis. Furthermore, in every field, in music, art, dance, sports, law, medicine, science, business, sociology, philosophy, communication, and every other aspect of life and society the Afrocentric critical methods start with the primary measure! Does it place Africans in the center? It proceeds on the basis of Haki's brilliant question, "Is it in the best interest of African peoples?" (Madhubuti, 1978).

The personalities and events most representative of our story in America and of the continent reflect our historical values; they teach us the nature of success and failure, good and evil, strength and weakness, what to hate and what to love. The lives of Piankhy, Tutankhamun, Nzingha, Tinubu, Hatshepsut, Isis, Horus, Tubman, Tutu, Asantewaa, Zumbi, Delaney, and Truth are just a few of the precious moments in our story which are as significant as the stories of Peter, Paul, Moses, Muhammad, Abu Bakr, Matthew, and David. Nothing is more right for you than the way derived from your own historical experiences. Whatever we know about the events surrounding the wars of England, the czars of Russia, the artistic flourishing in Italy; none of this knowledge is comparable to the knowledge you can have of yourself. Afrocentricity questions your approach to every conceivable human enterprise. It questions the approach you make to reading, writing, jogging, running, eating, keeping healthy, seeing, studying, loving, struggling, and working. If you do not come from an Afrocentric base, then you are in serious ethical and cultural trouble. No human being, who would be free, can be free by submitting when he does not have to submit. A fool is the person who cannot see that there are no longer any chains around his ankles, yet he walks as if he has weights at the bottom of his legs.

Our language must begin to reflect the new dimension to our struggle. Understand clearly that there is no *classical* music to you other than that which comes out of your culture. When a brother or sister says that Beethoven or Bach or Mozart is classical let us understand what is being said, they may be classical to Europeans but not to us. When the Europeans use classical they use it to refer to the highest of their art forms. To me, because of Afrocentricity, what they refer to is European Concert Music because the only classical music I know is the polyrhythms and syncopated eights or Ellington, Coltrane, Eubie Blake, Charlie Parker, Mingus, and Gillespie. I cannot deny the possibility of others speaking of classics within their contexts; I applaud their nationalism. I do not have to share in it when my tradition is so rich and varied. *Universal* is another of those words that has been used to hold the enemy in our brains. When a poet or a writer speaks on matters that relate to us, white critics are apt to say that the poet is not universal, meaning that he does not submit to white images or a Eurocentric framework. Such arrogance perceives the Afrocentric writer as narrow, but promotes the Eurocentric writer as universal. But we know where that comes from and understand precisely the nature of misleading classifications. A language mobilization constituting an Afrocentric sense begins and ends with consciousness.

You must be careful how you use language. Certain terms must either be redefined or eliminated. Consider the following list of terms that beg new definitions or elimination:

non-white	African slaves
tribe	hut
minority	cult
pygmy	mixed blood
jungle	primitive
war-like	colored
chief	Hottentot
headman	bushman
witch doctor	African slave trade
Black Death	African dialects
Black Africa	sub-Saharan
	native

To see how language can disrupt the thought of good solid brothers and sisters, ask one of your friends to comment on the meaning of these words. They should also be asked to find appropriate substitutes.

The Way of Newness

The poet is right when he says "we walk the way of the new world," a world built upon the foundations of political and cultural Afrocentricity. Nothing can ever achieve for us the victory we seek but a recapture of our own minds. Most Diasporan Africans and many continental African intellectuals have been taught by white teachers or by blacks who were taught by white teachers. White teachers cannot inspire in our children the visions necessary for them to overcome limitations. Walking the way of the new world means that we must establish schools which will teach our children how to behave like the kings and queens they are meant to be. It is the process of creating Afrocentric schools. Indeed, many of the "so-called" leaders must be re-educated, re-oriented, and restored to their center. The time for preachers who parade as leaders while taking our people down the sleepy road to a white Jesus who does little for our image or who participates in struggle against us is over. Afrocentricity says that "God" can speak to us as directly as he spoke to Nat Turner. It says that we do not have to rely upon the distant prophet of the Jews to give us God's words when we have prophets and holy people in our own heritage. We acknowledge that Jesus came among the Jews but we also recognize the presence of God among Africans and the wide acceptance of the Afrocentric view. The reason we walk the way of the new world is because as the express symbol for the survival of the spirit we have received the invaluable legacies of those who have gone before us and can now demonstrate the superiority of the way for us. It is superior for us because it is from us. It is not external to us; it was not given by some other people to us; it is not a paternalistic, materialistic, benevolent conceptualization. Afrocentricity is you. It derives from you and goes back to you. Now it is possible that your brain is so whitewashed that you cannot see your own center because of the white glare. A few students at a major university organized a splinter organization in opposition to the Black Student Union because they felt that the black students were much too involved in issues of Afrocentricity; they called their organization, Inter-race. Such madness is the direct consequence of self-hatred, obligatory attitudes, false assumptions about society, and stupidity. Our story does not afford us an example of genuine white obligation to anything that is African; it is healthy and is evidence of the respect with which they hold their own culture and heritage. No words can be strong enough for the person who undercuts his own salvation by engaging in rearguard actions for the enemy which strips him of his self-sense in the first place. Historically correct notions of cohesion and collective imperatives are the most instructive measures for us to assume at this time.

Our social scientists must begin to explore from an Afrocentric methodology the impact of racism on whites, and their socio-communication networks that inflict white racism upon them. Afrocentric social science may be a misnomer, what I am really saying is that Afrocentricity can be used to examine many aspects of white life with the intention of providing clues to successful intervention and circumvention. A total rewrite of the major events and developments in the world is long overdue. Let us give credit to Jacob Carruthers, Chancellor Williams, Ivan van Sertima, Yosef Ben-Jochannan, Maulana Karenga, and Cheikh Anta Diop. They have put us on our way. There has been and will be for the foreseeable future a need to examine the historical sources used by the white scholars to confute and refute the actual visual and textual evidences presented of the black civilization in Egypt. Our own research, lecturing, writing, and activism contribute to the restitution of the collective conscious will of Africa. When our will was broken, a dispersal of the most universal nature occurred. We had reached our point of technical perfection; our collective conscious will be lessened, and dissipated. I shall come back to this theme later. Nevertheless, the research to which we must address ourselves at this juncture has to do with recapturing our own collective consciousness. By reclaiming Egypt, deciphering the ancient writing of Nubia, circulating the histories and geographics of Ibn Khaldun and Ibn Battuta, and examining records of Africans in Mexico and other places in the new world, we have begun the necessary reconstruction.

Afrocentricity is the logical outgrowth of the collective conscious will of the people; the collective conscious will is derived from Afrocentricity. What seems like a tautology is. Afrocentricity and collective conscious will are one. It is impossible to have a people who accept one without accepting the other. However, it is possible for misguided persons to assume that they can have an Afrocentric collective consciousness through ideologies or religions external to their histories. What they have is a faith in some spookism! Why is it so difficult for us to believe in each other? People did not believe in the Honorable Elijah Muhammad, but they believed in Moses, Buddha, Jesus, Muhammad, and various Indian gurus. I believe that God spoke to many of our most active intellectuals, scholars, and teachers. The message they received was that all truth resides in our own experiences if we only look there.

Levels of Transformation

Afrocentricity is a transforming power which helps us to capture the true sense of our souls. There are five levels of awareness leading to transformation. The first level is called *skin recognition* which occurs when a person recognizes that his or her skin and/or her heritage is black but the person cannot grasp any further reality. The second level is *environmental recognition*. At this level, the person sees the environment as indicating his or her blackness through discrimination and abuse. The third level is *personality awareness*. It occurs when a person says "I like music, or dance, or chitterlings" and indeed the person may be speaking correctly and truthfully but this is not Afrocentricity. The fourth level is *interest-concern*. This level accepts the first three levels and demonstrates interest and concern in the problems of blacks and tries to deal intelligently with the issues of the African people. However, it lacks Afrocentricity in the sense that it has not become a commitment to an Afrocentric cultural base. *Afrocentric awareness*, the fifth level, is when the person becomes totally changed to a conscious level of involvement in the struggle for his or her own mind liberation. Only when this happens can we say that the person is aware of the collective conscious will. An imperative of will, powerful, incessant, alive, and vital, moves to eradicate every trace of powerlessness. Afrocentricity is like rhythms; it dictates the beat of your life.

New criteria for life emerges. People do not speak any longer about how many restaurants, how many movie theaters, how many factories a city has, but does a city have schools controlled by Afrocentricists, a museum, bookstore, a documentary center, and a cultural-spiritual gathering place which houses all the arts? Does a village have good health services? These become the yardstick by which communities are measured for and by African people. We are seriously in battle for the future of our culture; Afrocentric vigilance is demanded to preserve our culture. Politicians must no longer be allowed to speak in grand terms about employment and housing until they have addressed the value and spiritual issues which continue to plague the community. Thus, we see that Afrocentric awareness is greater than the other levels of awareness because they are merely stages toward perfection, not perfection itself. Once you have Afrocentric awareness no one needs to tell you that you have it or ask you if you have it; it is consciously revealed to yourself and those who meet you. You wear it on your face, in our walk and dress. By contrast, skin recognition is the lowest level of awareness because one only has to exist for it to be experienced. It is the brother we know who lives day by day without considering what he is meant to be or how damaging his life is to the collective will of the people. It is the sister who understands that she is black because she was born black but does not know what it really means. These are the people who are so easily victims of the environmental recognition factor. After they know that they are black in color, they may begin to experience and associate certain phenomena with blackness. In this way, Fanon understood that we could readily associate our difficulties with the social environment caused by our difference, that is, one could see discrimination as inherent in certain societies. Personality awareness is one of the most common levels. It occurs when the brother or sister only talks black, acts black, dances black, and eats black, but does not think black. Similarly, the person who demonstrates interest and concern by writing about blacks, speaking on blacks, and reporting blacks to whites has not achieved the full level of Afrocentric awareness. The person who refuses to condemn mediocrity and reactionary attitudes among Africans for the sake of false unity neither honors nor practices Afrocentricity. As the actions of racists can often be predicted with Afrocentric certainty, the actions of non-Afrocentric persons are also predictable.

At the interest-concern level of awareness a person may find opportunity to be involved in demonstrations against oppression, activities in support of African liberation, conferences about racism, and collecting funds for various worthy causes in the African community, but this is not Afrocentric awareness. It is most definitely an awareness but is has not reached the level of commitment to cultural reconstruction one finds n Afrocentric awareness.

Indeed culture is the most revolutionary stage of awareness, that is, culture in the sense that Amilcar Cabral, Frantz Fanon, and Maulana Karenga have written about. This is at the macro-level of education, and includes science, music, engineering, architecture, dance, art, philosophy, and economics. When we move away from an Eurocentric framework we become more innovative. We know that it is difficult to create freely when you use someone else's motifs, styles, images, and perspectives. Thus, the Afrocentric awareness is the total commitment to African liberation anywhere any everywhere by a consistent determined effort to repair any psychic, economic, physical, or cultural damage done to Africans. It is further a pro-active statement of the faith we hold in the future of African itself.

Consciousness

There are two aspects of consciousness: (1) toward oppression, and (2) toward victory. When a person is able to verbalize the condition of oppression, he exhibits the earliest consciousness of his oppression. This is the most elemental form of consciousness and is found in the speeches, poems, plays and lives of a million people who parade as conscious individuals. They know neither the correct expression of consciousness nor the damage they do to their own persons by practicing a fractured consciousness. In fact, they are often admired as being examples of conscious individuals. Thus, you have a sister saying in a seminar that "the white man will never let us be free; he's evil and we know it." She is conscious of oppression but not of victory. Or the brother who wrote the play with the slaves being whipped on the ship's decks, or the entertainer who gives time to the local church that fights against racism, or the poem that sings of "our intractable sorrow" or the young child who recognizes the differences between economic positions of her parents and the white parents.

I can know what is going on with the society and yet not know how to get out of a predicament. General knowledge is no substitute for specificity. The high schooler who wears corn rows or writes stories about black people may exhibit a consciousness of oppression but that is not consciousness of victory; consequently, deliverance is postponed until there is a victorious historical will.

The victorious attitude shows the Africans on the slave ship winning. It teaches that we are free because we choose to be *free*. Our choice is the determining factor, no one can be your master until you play the part of slave. A mighty victorious consciousness grounded in Afrocentricity is needed to create the national imperative. Speak victoriously, dispense with resignation, create excellence, and establish victorious values. Know your history and you will always be wise. The Africans on the slave ships won in more ways than they lost. Affection, courage, and humor in their pain were the elements which gave us the right to be new people today. No example of oppression consciousness is stimulating in a progressive sense. Our history and future are only connected in victory. Struggle itself becomes oppression consciousness when one cannot see the victory.

These two aspects of consciousness are both a part of our history. Like all history, we can speak of objective and subjective dimensions to our history. The type of relationship between our consciousness and our history is the true character of Afrocentricity. If we are Afrocentric, then we know that objective and subjective while not arbitrary designations are not ironclad. We determine what constitutes objectivity and subjectivity by deciding what is necessary in order for the relationship between history and consciousness to work. If a person does not know that the true character of a people resides in how they relate their history to the present and future. No Afrocentric person can ever have merely a consciousness of oppression, pain, and suffering. The present and future must be projected as victory, indeed the present must be lived victoriously. To be conscious of how difficult the European has made one's life is to be conscious at a very elemental level. It is like waking from a long sleep. When you first awake, you might rub your eyes or try to focus on some close object until your eyes clear. Consciousness of victory is the awareness that all attitudes and behaviors are achievable. Such a will overpowers any obstacle in your way and restores the Afrocentricists to strength. Strength is an inner attribute which cannot be bestowed by another.

Relationships

Njia teaches that man and woman are equally the source of our strength and indeed our genius. Because of this it is possible to discuss the nature and place of relationships within an Afrocentric philosophy. There are four aspects to Afrocentric relationships: *sacrifice, inspiration, vision,* and *victory*. In each of these aspects, we see elements of mutual respect and sharing. Sacrificial means that each partner is willing to give up certain aspects of himself or herself for the advancement of the people. Thus, the relationship is taken out of the individual context and placed into the collective context becoming a part of the generative will of the people, than it should be beneficial for me. Every man should want his lady to be Isis, Harriet, Yaa Asantewaa and every woman should want a Turner, Malcolm, Elijah, Muhammad, King, Garvey. The truth of the matter is that whatever is necessary for the collective will of the people must be done. A man and a woman willing to sacrifice the mundane things of society will find a full life in Afrocentricity. It means that sometimes you cannot be involved in the elementary existential manifestations of a decadent worldview. Afrocentricity is not anti-fun; it is for the creation of a new era in excitement and joy. Our creative wills in music, art, poetry, dance, and literature; our productive capacities in science, technology, and industry constitute the fun for us. A woman's time to create and a man's time to produce must be looked upon as a giving to the collective will. But like all sacrifices, Afrocentric sacrifice never really leaves us less. What seems to be a sacrifice always rebounds to happiness and joy. It gives us more than we had before.

Although there is danger that some people will try to pimp off of sacrifice, it must be understood that material considerations alone do not make a relationship; spirituality, collective cognitive imperatives, make relationships. A little more flowers, a few more gifts, a ring, an expensive trip do not make a relationship. Karenga is correct to see it merely as the cash connection. Understand that the person who pimps sacrifice will not be able to withstand the battle-fire. Ultimately, the test of sacrifice is the willingness to be Afrocentric everywhere and at all costs. It is a spiritual force at one with all the spirituality of the world; therefore, it is universal in itself. Our contribution to the nature of the male-female relationship must grow as everything we do, out of our experience as a people. The repository of that experience expands daily. Ceaseless vigilance of a determined victorious orientation must stamp out pimps who misuse relations.

The Afrocentric relationship is also inspirational. You are stimulated by your interactions with your partner, not just physically, but emotionally, psychologically, and intellectually as well. Our history teaches us that when this is not the case relationships falter. If you have one person who is always giving and another who is always receiving, the relationship is not satisfying. The man and woman in a relationship must be attuned to the primary objective of all Afrocentric unions: the productive and creative maintenance of the collective cognitive imperative.

Now that I have mentioned this collective cognitive imperative several times, what does it mean? It is the overwhelming power of a group of people thinking in the same direction. It is not unity in the traditional sense of a group of people coming together to achieve a single purpose; it is a full spiritual and intellectual commitment to a vision which constitutes the collective cognitive imperative. When we have a man and a woman as the smallest unit of society committed to the Afrocentric worldview we have one link in the spiritual chain. That link determines the future of the collective cognitive imperative by being an exact indication of the status of our will. Inspiration does not come from the sky, it comes from active thought and interaction. God is in you, not outside of you. When the ancient African priests in Egypt, the Yoruba priests in Nigeria, the Macumba priestesses of Brazil spoke or were possessed, their power was created by the generative will of mind. You can do the same thing if you are in contact with your god-force. This is, however, no easy task and that is precisely why Du Bois said only ten percent would suffice. Give us 250,000 conscious and willful Afrocentricists and a revolution will take place in our attitudes and behavior. The inspired man and woman or the man who inspires his lady and the lady who inspires her man must believe in the appointed destiny of the people. It is a destiny appointed by us, and consummated in our dynamic thrust toward the future. Each relationship's inspiration must be to make Afrocentrists out of others. Thus, it is just not much the giving of 250,000 people who are conscious as the making of 250,000.

Total conversion of the current population to Afrocentricity is not necessary. What is necessary is the persistent pressure of the Afrocentricists on other relationships to create in art, literature, science, music, etc., in order to counteract the reign of intellectual deviation among our creative people. Relationships which are based upon more than one or more than one woman can also be based upon the principles of Afrocentricity. While the couple is recognized as the most effective relationship in most cases, Njia does not prescribe form but it does prescribe content. People must inspire each other toward correct and righteous Afrocentricity. If she or he does not, then this is reason to raise serious questions about the practicability of the union. People do change; elements of future or potential change should be clearly discernible before you enter the relationship.

Do the people dream of what can be and how it can be done? A visionary aspect must appear in the relationship. The ability to plan for the future on the basis of a religious commitment to the Afrocentric worldview is the criterion of vision. Nothing can substitute for the visionary experience; it is the galvanizing element that keeps the relationship on track. To be able to ask, do you see and be assured that your partner does see the same vision provides a sense of communion. Commitment to a fundamental vision, a profound project, a spiritual quest, is the king of commitment which demonstrates vision. Relationships which are based on Afrocentric vision are never boring, dull, or without vitality. A visionary aspect to a relationship establishes a purpose outside of and beyond the daily considerations of living. The man and woman who dream together constitute the most advanced unit of an Afrocentric society.

What we must see in our visions are the victories of Afrocentricity. Its enlightened shadow must be made to cast itself upon all who interact with the couple. As visionaries, they must plan for the creation of schools, factories, laboratories, institutes, and centers. Visionaries do not simply work for others, they extend what they find. Anyone can walk into a store and start selling books, but to make the store something different than when you started working is the key to your vision. Anyone can teach, but not everyone can build a curriculum or a school. The visionaries say we shall do such and such and believe that it will be done because all things are possible. Afrocentricity should not be contradictory to your vision in a relationship. You should not have to be compartmentalized and say I'll do this and that there. Your whole center determines your effective vision and our vision relates back to your center. Thus, they become one. Sometimes a brother or sister gives the impression that he or she shall have to find time to be Afrocentric or find time to have vision. This is a deviation. Routine living should not be allowed to interfere with creative living. While it is true that couples often engage in this compartmentalization which dictates events, affections, situations, and activities for them around personal separateness; this is a dangerous fractionalizing practice.

Perhaps most significant of all is the fact that Afrocentric love is victorious. A celebration of ourselves, our aspirations, achievements, and accomplishments accompany the victorious aspect of a relationship. It is a relationship of joy, of power, of peace, of overcoming; it does not speak of failure or losses, of suffering and oppression. Victory means that you have won, not that you are expecting to win. Afrocentric relationships are victorious by their nature. Being Afrocentric is being victorious. When a woman finds a man who has achieved Afrocentricity, she has found a victor. The same is true for the man. Thus, both of them can create on the basis of their victory. Certain expressions like "we can't," "you ought not," "it is impossible," and "we're not equipped to" are anathema to the victorious relationship. We say more exactly, which means more Afrocentrically, we can do it.

Victory is important because it bestows on the relationship and those participating in it a sense of importance. The woman can be Isis, Nzingha, Yaa Asantewaa, and Harriet; they are all in Afrocentric history and are products of interactions with the ancestors in our history. Ours is a victorious history anyway; however you look at it. In fact, it is the longest running history on the face of the earth, having been interdicted seriously and at length only three times, namely, with the Greek penetration of Eastern Africa in 332 B.C., the Arab penetration of Eastern Africa in 640 A.D., and the rise of the European exploitation in the 15th Century. The latter interdiction covered East, West, and South Africa. European footnotes to our history can cause us to lose sight of our victorious nature. Couples must underscore their participation in the great drama of our history by demonstrating a love which can transcend the mundane activities of a relationship. Love is victory. But understand that the true Afrocentric love is found only in the context of the profound cause; otherwise it degenerates into a spectacle of buying and selling. What is one more diamond ring if there is no sense of destiny, not togetherness in a victorious union as an expression of the relationship? The answer is clearly nothing more than the meaningless play on rituals established to support the cash, flesh, or dependent connection. To get beyond this, we must seriously rise up in victory for Afrocentricity. This will reconstruct our families, reorganize our values, and protect our culture. The crisis in priority has produced the crisis in relationships. Never before in the history of the world have a people been so completely severed from their collective cognitive imperative. Such splintering has been the downfall of numerous nations and peoples; it has rendered us dull to the shock treatments of capitalist society as it tries to resurrect a corpse. Our people, without a collective will, enter relationships for all of the wrong reasons. That is not my immediate concern. Caught up in the collective will of Hollywood we fall victim too easily to an alien notion of what love is and how to achieve it. In a victorious union, we celebrate our Afrocentricity and grow in it each day. When we have achieved sacrifice, inspiration, vision, and victory we realize that we have accomplished all the elements of an Afrocentric relationship. From this fountain flows all the good that we do for each other and the people. It is never unconnected from the life of the people because to be together as one is to be together as one with others as well as with another. Our Afrocentricity expands in relationship to our involvement with the spiritual and intellectual forces within our own history. When a man and woman become related in a physical, emotional, and spiritual manner they are making history for the coming generation. Every act must be made with an ourstorical sense. When you introduce yourself to your lover, when you agree on things to do, when you work together on projects for the people, it must be with an Afrocentric base. Only this base allows you the kind of true identity with the past and future that each of us seeks. When the union of man and woman is victorious nothing can separate you from the love of the people; you are one with each other and consequently one with the people. It is an impossibility to be one with each other Afrocentrically and not be one with the people. The one who claims to love you but does not love the people is attempting to deceive you. This occurs most often when the person has deceived him or herself into believing that they can separate their love for you from their love of the people and still remain Afrocentric. This is not possible.

In order to get the brother she wanted a sister went through numerous outer changes of sartorial fashions, hairstyles, and manner of speech. After he had begun relating to her she ceased her outer changes and the relationship went from bad to worse. She accused him of not being interested in her for herself but because of her fashions and and styles. In this case both the brother and the sister had made some gross errors of judgment, errors which could not have been made if they had been Afrocentric. Indeed the sister felt that the brother would naturally respond to her display of outward symbols of Afrocentricity; she was correct in this assumption because all people automatically respond to the elements of spirit in our heritage. However, the brother, not being Afrocentric although aware of the outer changes and possibilities, was seduced by superficialities. Neither was satisfied because neither came from their centers which start with the people as all encompassing and all embracing.

The people are the source and inspiration for all that the couple do in word or deed. If they decide to build a factory, buy a building, or create a play, that sense of action must be rooted in the principles of *umoja*, unity, and *ujima*, collective work.

The Afrocentric drive to create must always be based on a deep collective commitment to excellence. Thus, Afrocentricity detests the conspiracy of unproductivity and generates the ability to handle problems by the will of our genius. When someone says, "Watu weusi ought to have a school," or "we ought to create a museum," or "we need to build a shoe factory," he has set the task for himself. You are the one who must do what you propose. If you say, "why don't we establish?" you have stated the responsibility for bringing the idea into being. Only then can we have the collective consciousness necessary to carry on the reconstruction of the world.

Homosexuality is a deviation from Afrocentric thought because it makes the person evaluate his own physical needs above the teachings of national consciousness. An outburst of homosexuality among black men, fed by the prison breeding system, threatens to distort the relationship between friends. While we must be sensitive to the human complexity of the problem as Haki Madhubuti counsels in *Enemies: The Clash of Races*, we must demonstrate a real antagonism toward those gays who are as unconscious as other people. In fact, black gays are often put in front of white or integrated organizations to show the liberalism of the group. These gays tend to live in the make-believe world of white gays. Our task in an Afrocentric vein is to give our sons and daughters healthy self-concepts. A male child needs encouragement in his activities. The child must feel that his manhood is attached to a mind working on important questions.

The rise of homosexuality in the African-American male's psyche is real and complicated. An Afrocentric perspective recognizes its existence but homosexuality cannot be condoned or accepted as good for the national development of a strong people. It can be and must be tolerated until such time as our families and schools are engaged in Afrocentric instructions for males. White racism with its fangs claws at the soul of black manhood which results in an alteration of black womanhood as well. Afrocentric relationships are based upon sensitive sharing in the context of what is best for the collective imperative of the people. We can no longer allow our social lives to be controlled by European decadence. The time has come for us to redeem our manhood through planned Afrocentric action. All brothers who are homosexuals should know that they too can become committed to the collective will. It means the submergence of their own wills into the collective will of our people. Guard your minds and you shall save your bodies. An ideology of Afrocentricity is derived from our history and provides all the guidelines for action. The homosexual shall find the redemptive power of Afrocentricity to be the magnet which pulls him back to his center.

Afrology

Afrology is the Afrocentric study of concepts, issues, and behaviors with particular bases in the African world, diasporan and continental. Black Studies, African Studies, and African-American Studies are essentially afrological studies, that is, persons within departments or programs with such names are usually engaged in the Afrocentric study of concepts, issues and behaviors in the African world. Where this is not the case, you do not have afrology. Thus, another name for Black Studies, African Studies, or African-American Studies may be *afrology*. Of course, we recognize that such a coined term may work better in institutions in the Eurocentric world than it would or should in an Afrocentric world where the root of the word preferably should be derived from an African language. As Wangui wa Goro would say, "Using our own languages we would not have such problems."

The field of Black Studies or African-American Studies was not born from a clear ideological position in the 1960's. Our analyses as students were correct, but our solutions were often fragmentary, ideologically immature, and philosophically ill-defined. The absence of a comprehensive philosophical position, with attendant possibilities for a new logic, science, and rhetoric condemned us to experimentation with an Islamic base, a Marxist base, a civil service base, a reactionary nationalist base, a social service base, a systematic nationalist base, or a historical-cultural base. Systematic nationalists tended to be grouped with the historical-cultural school because they, at least, understood that Black Studies implied a different perspective although they could never thoroughly articulate that perspective.

Afrocentricity as that perspective becomes indispensable to our understanding of Black Studies; otherwise, we have a series of intellectual adventures in Eurocentric perspectives about Africans and African-Americans. That is why the students of the sixties, in their moment of intellectual purity which remained uncaptured until now, railed against white instructors of Black Studies. As we now know the mistake was not in their intention: to have a black perspective (they did not refer to it as Afrocentricity) but it was in their misunderstanding that Afrocentricity meant black professors. The complainers who decried the existence of such a radical intellectual movement have etched a footnote for themselves in our history. Their opposition to the heroic academic act of the students and advanced scholars can only be regarded as the reaction of the fearful. Scared that they might think of another frame of reference, they opposed the establishment of our collective consciousness. These professors demonstrated how easy it is for Africans to have Eurocentric reference points.

The outlines of an Afrocentric base for scholarship are rooted in the social, political, and economic values of our people. We recognize that the care begins with African-Americans who, because of the special process of "de-tribalization and re-tribalization" into Africans, have stepped over the boundaries of ethnicity in order to reformulate the African view of the world. No uniqueness accrues to African-Americans because of this history except as it relates to viewing the continent. As products of African amalgamation (Hausa, Asante, Yoruba, Ewe, Ibo, Wolof, Mandingo, Congo, and a hundred other ethnic groups) and the American crucible we have become a new people unknown prior to the 15th Century, our perspectives, attitudes, and experiences are peculiarly fitted to change the frame of reference for African people. Not until we are able to look within our own value systems for intellectual and spiritual guidance will we be capable of redressing our own worldview and thereby modifying our behavior. Afrology, as a field of study, promises to be the instrument we need and by definition it possesses an Afrocentric base.

This knowledge inspires our scholars, galvanizes our artists, and liberates our philosophers. A revitalized scientific and artistic tradition will emanate from our people once the perspective, Afrocentricity, is understood and accepted by the creative and recreative minds of our people. It will not be possible for scholarship to advance without reference to our center. This guarantees a reclamation of the correct values for liberation (Padmore, 1972).

The Method

Afrology is the crystallization of the notions and methods of black oriented social scientists and humanists. What they had explained, analyzed, and promulgated in papers, lectures and private conversations has taken shape, which is one with substance, as a new, creative discipline squarely resting on the foundations of our African past. Perhaps no other area of inquiry in modern times has been born with so many attendants, some obviously waiting around to throw the baby out with the bath water but others firmly determined to nourish the nascent discipline to full maturity. Afrological logic is a singular academic achievement. It has made possible the conceptualization of black perspectives and attitudes, thereby suggesting a new methodology.

However, there will continue to be problems in analysis, until we have concretized the proper investigatory procedures and analytic formulas. Some of our premises have been confused with those of other disciplines and have thereby caused considerable mis-interpretations. *Afrology* is not merely the study of black people, but an approach, a methodological and functional perspective. Black people have been the subjects of numerous studies but those studies have not been Afrocentric in method.

It is popular nowadays to call up the deeds of W.E.B. Du Bois, E. Franklin Frazier, Carter G. Woodson, Benjamin Brawley, Alain Locke and other scholars as indications of a long and distinguished history in afrology. But this is to invoke the names of the ancestors amiss. They were scholars who studied our people but seldom afrologists. This is why I have said that afrology is a crystallization of notions and methods, it is the being of what was coming to be in the perceptions and perspectives of these great men. In almost every case they were excellent historians, critics, and sociologists but not Afrologists. And the fact that black people were studied in the past by other black people does not mean that the perspectives were Afrological. Furthermore, not all blacks are capable of being Afrologists because it is neither a matter of color nor theme that determine one's expertise as a Afrologist. *It is the Afrocentric method which makes Afrological study.*

There are three basic qualities possessed by Afrologists: (1) *competence*, (2) *clarity of perspective*, and (3) *understanding of the object.* Competence includes the analytic skills with which the scholar investigates his subject. It is the ability and capability of performing adequately when confronted with problems related to his subject area. Competence may be acquired through formal training, if available, experience or a combination of both. Further, the competence of a person in one area does not automatically transfer to another. Thus a good historian or sociologist is not necessarily a good afrologist. Clarity of perspective means the ability to focus on the Afrocentric issues in the subject area and to interpret those issues in a way that will expose the essential factors constituting the subject. In afrology this means that the scholar who has a clear perspective, say, of the Watts uprising does not interpret it as a riot. He sees the political implications inherent in the phenomenon and would therefore consider alternative designations such as rebellion or uprising or protest. Understanding the subject means that the scholar knows something of the interrelationship of his subject and the world context. He approaches the subject in relationship to the world at large and is able to analyze the phenomena occurring in and around the subject, the parts comprising the subject, and the events constituting an Afrocentric focus of study. In the case of the afrologist, the subject of study is definitionally related to people of African descent. But it does not mean that anyone studying Africans is an afrologist; furthermore, as I have intimated before, a black person studying English literature may be a scholar, but not an afrologist by the virtue of his scholarship. If he studies English literature Afrocentrically, he becomes an afrologist.

What I hope to provide in the following discussion are two theoretical propositions that will set the tone for an analysis of the discipline as it is becoming. This becoming will be concomitant with the rise of Afrocentricity, which is its core. *The first proposition is that afrology is primarily pan-Africanist* in its treatment of the creative, political, and geographic dimensions of our collective will to liberty. It is a discipline which underscores the relationship of black people from various parts of the world, and as such organizes our thoughts and ideas into a composite whole. What we believe intuitively is verified by afrological methods; what our ancestors discovered about herbs, human personality, music, and religion is found to be valid or invalid by afrologists. Those concepts that were detrimental to our survival as free people are exposed and eliminated. In this sense afrology opens the door to our true selves; whatever there is that is negative in our persons is measured by a new formula; and whatever is positive is also measured by a new formula; and whatever is positive is also measured by the same Afrocentric formula. The questions, then, of how we walk, or how we talk, or what colors we like, our mode of production, or how we dance, are all submitted to afrologists, who, as I have indicated, possess the proper qualities to make an assessment. As we look more closely at this proposition, it is obvious that the creative dimension is, also, pan-Africanist. Some of our poets and musicians have long since begun to see connections and have frequently returned to meditate at the roots of the baobob of history. They are bold in their declarations because their arts *stand up* out of the midst of troubles and sorrow to pronounce our resurrection. No longer will our art mimic white art and be separate from the people; it will retouch the essence of our souls and be spirit and body, force and energy, shape and sound. The *Nommo* of these coming artists is pan-Africanist, defined by acceptance of the past, with a different consciousness, augmented by Afrology as a discipline, and therefore significantly productive.

Before Du Bois' Pan-African Congress in Paris, the movement for black intellectual understanding, that is, the framing of proper political questions for Africans had been accorded only a small space in our history. Since that time we have incorporated the best thinking of Du Bois, Kwame Nkrumah, Malcolm X, Frantz Fanon, George Padmore, and Marcus Garvey to fuel the philosophical discussions of afrology. Dynamic perception, based upon an essentially African worldview, establishes the focus of our intellectual task. Politically we have moved beyond one dimensional perception to multi-dimensional perception, taking in many nations' conditions but always relating them back to the fundamental perspective of Africa. The Continent is where it all began and it makes little or no sense to talk about politics apart from the political evolutions in Africa. Because we have begun to develop and nourish the African perspective it gets harder to get white answers to our questions. Pan-Africanism itself is a political perspective and a political ideology as well as a social theory. The one does not negate the other. Actually when we speak of the political dimensions of the concept we are also talking about how Africans see themselves as social units. There are, of course, variant positions on these questions as on others among Africans but Afrocentricity points to a closer, more earnest endeavor to effect substantive changes in our role in the world. But this is not all.

We cannot discuss Pan-Africanism without reference to Afro-America in a geographic sense. By Afro-America we mean the domicile of people of African descent in the Americas. Our concern is not simply the United States, but includes Brazil, Venezuela, Columbia, Ecuador, Peru, Mexico, Central America, and the West Indies. Over 40% of the new world Africans live in Brazil, 37% live in the United States. Any study of afrology, however, must consider the total geographical distribution of Africans. As an inclusive discipline, afrology brings together our creative, political, and geographic dimensions as a Pan-Africanist reality. Herein lies the future of the field.

A second proposition is that the afrologist, by virtue of his perspective, participates in the coming to be of new concepts and directions. His perceptions of political and social reality allow him to initiate novel approaches to problems and issues. Without the Western point of view he is mentally as free as possible. This is not a closed path; it is open to all who would change their perspectives. In fact, the afrologist, typically, is a person who is capable of understanding many points of view because he values such diversity of opinion. He may change his perspective by altering his conditions, or because of some external influences on the object perceived but the perception is always uniquely his. For example, whereas a white communication scholar may define a speech a an uninterrupted spoken discourse given before an audience; an afrologist looking at the same object, a speech, would possibly derive a different definition. The reason for this is because his definition must reflect his experiences and Afrocentric point of view. Definitions are contextual. Thus the afrologist might say that a speech is a *highly interrupted* spoken discourse. Given this definition he would be emphasizing the extent to which the conventional black speech depends upon audience participation. He knows that in the black cultural audiences the speakers are interrupted by shouts of "amen," "hallelujah," and "right on." Further the afrologist would demonstrate that these interjections are not interruptions at all but *affirmations* and that the speech cannot be complete without the interchange of vocal expressions. Antiphony becomes central to the black communicative process.

Certainly some white communicationists recognize this as a specific African form but because of the inability to escape the Eurocentric view, the white academic is often trapped when speaking of black communication phenomena. Here then is an example of why students have demanded that all teachers of Black Studies be black. Many administrators and professors thought this to be the height of intellectual arrogance. What the students were asking for, however, were those teachers who could deal with those concepts and ideas they knew were intuitively correct. The request for black professors was to maximize the probability that the professors would be sensitive to Afrocentricity. Of course, some white and some blacks reacted negatively. It must always be expected that those who see their perspective as the only one possible will respond negatively toward a competing perspective. There were more than academic feudal baronies at stake; philosophical perceptions were also being questioned. The advent of a new perspective is a rupturing event, because it introduces different concepts into the learning place. Yet it is not the difference that produces the rupture; academics contend that they thrive on difference. It is the apparent antagonism of the African worldview that causes many academics to shudder. They are wary when an afrologist challenges the validity of their measures, or advises them on the proper and improper questions to be raised about social life. Unquestionably this was the principal bone of contention for many colleges and universities; they perceptively understood that the introduction of Black Studies would challenge some of the traditional assumptions about education and society.

However, many students did not see the fallacy of color as a criterion for teaching afrology. Despite the essential soundness of our philosophy in recognizing the need to appoint professors sensitive to our heritage and history, we failed to see that some blacks were not capable of being afrologists. Degrees from universities are not indications of one's capabilities, that is, one's sensitivity and responsiveness to black cultural data. In fact, there are some black professors who would, because of their total baptism in Western perspectives, argue that there exists no particular black cultural data. Appointment of such black professors to universities made little difference to the conventional education process; some of these professors were often beguiled by their status and therefore added no new insights into traditional disciplines. Students who demanded black professors quickly discovered that race did not determine her sensitivity. The true criterion, then, is not color but Afrocentricity. Clearly, then, a scholar possessing the essential qualities outlined above may be an afrologist, and thereby participate in the advent of innovations in education.

Now we are prepared to ask, what is the future of Afrology as a discipline? It is well to recall that disciplines have a way of changing from one thing to another indicating special emphasis or need. Rhetoric, at one time essential to early American education, has since given birth to various offspring: Oral English, Speech and Drama, Speech, Speech Communication and Communication Studies. In every instance there has been a link, a connection with the previous emphasis. So the answer to the question begins with an understanding that all disciplines stimulate the educational process and are in turn stimulated by it. More than this, of course, is the external stimuli that help to determine the disciplinary focus and emphasis.

Afrology, has impacted on scholarship in a remarkable way by drawing its vital energies, insights, concepts, and ideas, from the particular experiences of African people. In the future, afrology shall take these vital energies to a new level of consciousness. That is, there will be a concentrated effort to explore the various behavioral and cultural leads given by past and contemporary scholars. The influence of afrology on conventional education will open the latter to what Harold Cruise has called "pluralistic perspectives."

The discipline is now permanently realized in academia and will multiply throughout the African continent and its diaspora. Research has issued forth like a river to form an irrepressible development. My belief is that progressive universities will continue to make a place for the discipline, actually augmenting existing programs with experimental research components. Since afrology is based upon an Afrocentric interpretation and a particular conception of society, the results of our work will alter previous perceptions and set standards for future studies of African peoples. It is here that afrology comes into its own as an organizing methodology, and therefore proper, consciousness of cultural and historical data. Such a proper consciousness is founded upon the genuine acceptance of our African past, without which there is no Afrological discourse or basis for peculiar analysis. We are therefore participants in the coming transformation of education, a transformation appropriately prompted by the evolutionary discipline of Afrology.

Confraternity and Continuum

Despite the fact that a great many African-Americans know next to nothing about African life, Africa is the most prevailing symbol in African-American mythology. Our writers and poets have frequently invoked the sacred name of the continent as a symbol of all our aspirations and strivings. Marcus Garvey was the most provocative Diasporan proponent of Africa in this century. To him there was no substitute symbology for the African. So the psychical and physical migrations of African-Americans have always taken Africa as a symbol. Because of the intense and magnetic attraction of Africa the question of the African confraternity is most relevant. What concerns me in this discussion is the place of Africa as a real and imaginary factory in the rediscovery of our past which shall escort the rise of our spirit into the next generation. There are several dimensions to such an exposition. In one instance we can speak about the African continuum as an influential element in the acceptance of the past. In another we could concern ourselves with the work of African writers on the subject of *Négritude* and the African Personality. And in still another vein we could be drawn to see the interaction between Africa and Europe in the cultural context with an aim toward the explication of Africa as a magnetic symbol. These are the tasks I shall undertake with the added endeavor to show where the confraternity will go in the coming rise of the spirits.

The recognizable modalities of black Americans constitute a continuum from Africa to the New World. In the words of Baraka there exists an "epic memory" that supports the African-American thrust into America. It is a deep remembrance of habits, styles, mannerisms, and behaviors which reflects itself in language, music, and people customs. The relationship between coastal West African languages and the language of blacks in the West Indies and the American South has been demonstrated more than once. Lorenzo Turner's *Africanisms in the Gullah Dialect* (1948) was among the first linguistic classics dealing with black language. Turner shows that four thousand expressions used by blacks in South Carolina and Georgia are traceable to African languages. Furthermore, while some expressions were more common than others, all of them were identifiable by the respondents. In other studies, Turner pointed out that these expressions were not mispronounced English words as some white critics charged but authentic African vocabulary items. One link, then, between Africa and America is evidenced in language. *We are African peoples* and the consequent developments of our spirits are not just indicative of the past but the essence of our adaptive behavior toward the West. Another aspect of our African linguistic contribution has been our vocal tonality which when mixed with European tones gave the South its distinctive speech pattern. This phenomenon did not occur elsewhere primarily because the density of Africans in the United States was nowhere else equal to that of the Deep South. So the impact of blacks on the white behavioral patterns of the American South was a direct result of the African continuum.

There is even a more telling characteristic of African continuity in language than the retention of certain vocabulary items. We can find numerous words derived from Africa, "goober," "biddy," "okra," "o.k.," "agogo," etc., but not all of us have knowledge of Africanisms in our speech. Is there therefore no trace of the "epic memory" in our speech? For most of us, even if we do not use African vocabulary items, the touch of Africa is present. By this, I mean that our very expressiveness represents an African style. When someone says "he sure can rap," or "he sure sounded good." The responder is affirming the presence of the continuity in that person. Thus, how we say something is co-equal with what we say. Both are important. Although people may accept what a person says because of the intrinsic worth of the ideas, the message would be more powerful if it was also well spoken. To be well spoken implies tone, gesture, rhythms, and a bit of styling.

Perhaps it is in music that we have seen our most authentic example of continuity. Unquestionably the spirituals which are synonymous with elegant art, the blues which speak our essential pathos, and jazz which suggests all the intricate ways we create and communicate are the legacies of our epic memories. The musical forms represent a continuous linkage with the rituals and performance arts of West Africa. Because music sits astride our traditions, it will monitor our future. Whatever happens in economics, politics, and society will be engaged by our musicians; they are both leaders and followers. The idea of engaging the various developments highlights the reciprocity inherent in the artistic context. If an innovation occurs in politics, the musicians will engage it in art. On the other hand our politicians have frequently tried to realize the concepts present in our music. James Brown, the king of soul music, has preached "get on the good foot" and our politicians have understood the meaning of that tune. Brown is an energizer, one is inclined to say he is a soul-giver, whose music bursts forth from our collective emotions. He sings what millions of voices would sing if given the opportunity to express themselve, that is precisely the strength of his appeal. But while James Brown has established an essentially urban African-American sound with roots in the rhythm and blues field, he is not a traditional blues singer. When we listen to the earthy realism, say, of Huddie "Leadbelly" Ledbetter in "The Bourgeois Blues" or the powerful verses of Jimmy Witherspoon's "Tell Him I Was Flyin'," we experience the line, the direct track from Africa to Lightnin' Hopkins and Jimmy Cain. All the elemental passions are aroused in the rhetoric of Bessie Smith, Billie Holiday, Big Bill Broonzy, and John Lee Hooker. What is basic to our life is captured in our art. Fela and Sonny Ade in Nigeria show us how much we are one spirit.

Central to the revitalization of the African in America is the coming age of international travel, particularly to Africa which shall expand the borders of our politics. Here I see the most direct involvement of African-Americans in Africa and a consequent energizing of Afrocentricity. The contact phenomenon is inestimable but certainly the relationship between Africans and Afro-Americans will not only be material but will also be emotional. There are some people around who argue that Africans and African-Americans have nothing in common but the color of their skin. This is not merely an error, it is nonsense. There exists an emotional, cultural, psychological connection between this people that spans the oceans and the separate existence. It is in our immediate responses to the same phenomena, it is how we talk, how we greet, how we style, the essential elements of our habitual behavior. We are not African-Americans without Africanity; we are an African people, a new ethnic group to be sure, a composite of many ancient people, Asante, Efik, Serere, Touculur, Mande, Wolof, Angola, Hausa, Ibo, Yoruba, Dahomean, etc. And quite frankly our politics, like the expressiveness our religion, is more often similar in sentiment to that of Africa than of white America. Not surprisingly, when we sympathize and participate in the struggle to liberate South Africa and Namibia, we feel their anger at the arrogance of racism. We have always felt that South Africa had to be free and we have always abhorred the United States' investments in that racist country. In this respect our international politics resembles that of the African nations more than that of the United States. Thus the fabric of our political behavior is woven together with the universal plight of Africans. And it is because of our acceptance of the past that we shall teach our African brothers the lessons three hundred and fifty years of exile have taught us.

What seems clear is that our brothers have too easily taken the past for granted or have refused to honor the ancestors in whose paths we must trod. The past escapes if it is not understood, clarified, and constantly interpreted in the light of new revelations. Reclamation is no simple task; it is, in fact, fraught with untold dangers. Our success has been due to an unusually active leadership which emphasized the importance of roots. Some people have missed the point of departure and have come up with various manners of beliefs, organizations, and cults. That we are becoming more conscious of Africa, then, is an accepted fact; that we have struggled to see that our acceptance not generate into false price or empty glory-saying is commendable. We are by reckoning of our acceptance in a fit position to analyze the areas in which we shall have a closer fraternity with continentals.

As we continue to travel, the influence on continentals will be much greater than their influence on us. I speak here of contemporary, not historical, influences dictated by status, wealth, and education. There are yet no large and diverse groups of Africans who travel throughout the African New World. Undoubtedly, some would like to do so; and there are elite classes who do, but actually, other than students, there are not yet many continentals travelling to the diaspora. On the other hand, African-Americans are now acquiring the means for international travel and the first place they usually go is Africa. At one time it would have been Europe, but now almost three-fourths of the African-Americans who travel make Africa their first stop.

This influx of African-Americans will have an increasingly powerful impact on Africans who will begin to participate in the new world African culture. What occurs in this instance is the return to Africa, in a diluted form, of African presence and the interaction of Africans with that created form. Diasporic influence, then, initially takes shape in aesthetics and matters of style. In the areas of clothing, fashions, hairstyles, and expressive behaviors in language, the African-American influence becomes significant. Indeed, our aesthetic impact has become international, and can be found from Mexico to Japan. Nevertheless, our African influence remains fundamental to our discussion here. For example, in the field of music our artists are generally much better known in African than African artists are in America. But it is the overpowering capacity of technology that distinguishes our ability to disseminate innovations. Technology will be the basis for spreading one's products in the present age. But further, it is not just the use that is important but by implication in the use, *availability*, is the cornerstone of dissemination. Quite certainly, Africans can create and use the instruments of technology as well as anyone but it is a question of possessing the material or human resources to give an artist access that accounts, to a greater extent than anything else, for the lack of the African artists' presence in the United States. In the case of sculpturing, we are now witnessing the popularity of the Nigerian master, Lamidi Fakeye, who is widely known in the United States and has demonstrated that this art speaks to African culture, and taught has broad applications in Black Studies departments. He stands as one of the most accomplished African sculptors of his century. In addition to Fakeye are the writers Soyinka, Beti, Ngugi, Aidoo, Mugo, and Okai; the musicians Masekela, Fela Kuti, and the master drummer Kwasi Badu. Stevie Wonder, James Brown, Michael Jackson, and Tina Turner are household words in the West African capitals. While African musicians such as Fela, Ade, Masakela, and Makeba, have penetrated the veil of the African-American audiences, they have yet, and it will come, to break through to the light.

In literature, on the other hand, we have seen the likes of Wole Soyinka, J. Pepper Clark, Camara Laya, Chinua Achebe, Cameron Duodu, Alex La Guma, Isidore Okpewho, Micere Mugo, Atukwei Okai, Ama Aidoo, Ngugi wa Thiong'o, Okot P'Bitek, and Kofi Awoonor rise to capture our souls. Literature is infinitely more easily transmitted from a viewpont of technics. Print does not depend so much on the machinery of dissemination; it is itself disseminatible as literature without a disc or a record player or various middlemen. The printed page is also more inexpensively disseminated than recorded music. Thus we know the African writers and will know them better when Afrocentricity becomes a reality for us; even white Americans, will seek to know the sense of the African soul.

What are the symbols of this connectedness between Africa and America? They are represented in the extension and exchange of personality and projects. Continentals know Malcolm X, King, Andy Young, Jesse Jackson, and we know Mugabe, Tommie Sankara, and Samora Machel. Chief M.K.O. Abiola, publisher of the *African Concord* magazine, sponsored an international Pan-African conference on the food crisis in Africa that demonstrated in an historic way how a private continental African could affect connectedness and extension.

The continent accepts diasporan athletes as its own because of the common origin and struggle against oppression. Akeem Olajuwon, the Nigerian basketball star, and Pele, the Brazilian, are popular figures in the African-American pantheon because of their Africanity. However, it would be a mistake to assume that celebrities offer the only avenue of exchange since both education and technology provide more important areas of interaction. Thus, Afrocentricity focuses our exploration on the African past in such a way as to encourage a rich interaction with Africa for our future.

Négritude

On another level, somewhat related, is the idea of *Négritude* expounded by African writers trying to explicate the peculiar dimensions of African personality. It is in this concept, or better still, the French speaking African intellectuals' treatment of this concept, that we get another indication of how the rise of black spirits will interact with Africans. The leaders of *Négritude* included Leon Damas, Leopold Senghor, Jacques Rabemananjara, and Aime Cesaire who conceptualized for the African and West Indian the response to European cultural imposition in the development of *Négritude* as a point of departure. Nothing transforms our self-concept like authentic confrontation. Cesaire, the greatest living poet, and Senghor, had just such realization to strike them while living in Paris, perhaps the European city most proud of its cultural heritage. They knew that what Europe admired was not the essence nor the emphasis of African culture and set out to write literature with African sensibilities. *Négritude* was an attempt to lay out in specific and general terms what constituted the foci of African culture. Alioune Diop provided the journal *Presence Africaine* as an outlet for the works of the *Négritude* writers. It must be understood, however, that in America our intellectuals and artists were expanding in a surrealistic way the boundaries of literature and music before the conceptualization of *Négritude*. What has been called the *Harlem Renaissance* was an anticipation of the *Négritude* movement in French-speaking African countries and of African Personality discussions in English-speaking countries, particularly in Ghana. The fullness of the time had not come for Afrocentricity in either of those movements; they were apologetic movements with gifted individuals attempting to justify our culture to the world. Nkrumah, more than any of his contemporary political colleagues, wanted to see our view translated into political power. Therefore, interaction suggested by cross-fertilization energizes the black American's acceptance of the past. There can be no true confraternity without the attraction of Africa as a symbol because to accept the past is to deal with Africa intellectually. And for the black American not to deal with Africa on an intellectual basis is to remain encapsulated, in effect, isolated from the African consociation.

The future course is clear. African confraternity inspired by a correct and positive afrology and resting upon the modalities and insights of the people will become a positive force. Alioune Diop, founder of *Presence Africaine*, wanted a firm connection between Africans on the Continent and in the Diaspora, and gave scholars such as Cheikh Anta Diop and John Henrik Clarke the opportunity to demonstrate this confraternity.

With the constant nurturing of black intellectuals and artists the confraternity will continuously address the masses and we will all respect the wills of our African ancestors and build upon their dreams the structure they envisioned. The perfecting of this consociation will only take place in the rise of the spirits. We seek to break out of our isolation and distance and come closer to our African brothers and sisters through a collective consciousness.

Christian Church

The black church is the single most authoritative religious force within our community. It is, furthermore, our only continuous anchor to the *orishas, loas* and ancestors of our past. Still more, the church has served both as dissuader and catalyst in our most necessary social and political struggles. Yet because it is seldom consciously Afrocentric, it is often a controversial institution. The nature of the controversy reveals the fundamental weakness of the church which unfortunately seems little altered by the debates over objectives, functions, and rituals. There has to be a general regeneration of the black church. Possibly, this renewal, might occur simultaneously with the foreseeable intellectual resurrection. Nonetheless, whether or not its transformation occurs in conjunction with a general black awakening, it must occur. Without the full participation of the church we cannot have a genuine re-creation. In fact, our history shows that the church, sooner or later, establishes itself as transmitter of the new visions within our community. The work of Albert Cleage, James Cone, and Cornel West in producing the groundwork for committing the churches to the collective consciousness is remarkable.

It is now possible to make an analysis of the church and then make some comments about its direction. First, while the church is the most dominant institution within the black community, it is not a united church in any political, social, or religious sense. It is, however, united symbolically as the black church; but the consequences of this fragmentation are not overcome by any reference to symbols. What then is the nature of the church's authority? It is the individual wills of the preachers that constitute the power of the church. Those who minister to the flock control not only the religion but the pocketbooks and the politics of the flock. It is the recognition of this fact alone which has traditionally brought old and new white politicians into the community to beg the preachers for votes.

The church leaders control more followers than all of the protest organizations. For example, there is no American civil rights organization that commands as many followers as the president of the black Baptists. Yet that president has never used that power to bring about an Afrocentric collective imperative. In any single community, while the various congregations are autonomous, the Baptists usually represent a considerable force. In much the same way the paramount Bishop of the African Methodist Episcopal Church is a formidable power. As leader of the oldest black institution, he commands the respect that comes with tradition and heritage. The history of the black protest movmenet in the nineteenth century, before and after emancipation, parallels the history of the American Methodist Episcopal Church. And while the A.M.E. has lost its nineteenth-century zeal it remains potentially productive, socially and politically. There are numerous other churches most controlled, either administratively or theologically, by white churches, e.g., Adventists, Churches of Christ, Jehovah Witnesses, Methodists, Episcopalians, etc. Yet, collectively, the church remains a force with which all pretenders to black power must reckon. These churches dispense favors, on the right people, like an old uncle gives candy to nice nieces and nephews. But like an old uncle the Christian church often refuses to see new realities, perhaps it cannot because of its own contradictions. A new consciousness would depose the church and institute Afrocentricity as the principal ideology.

Another aspect of the church community is the indigenous Christian movements. These lively and colorful original religious activities further reflect the pervasiveness of the church. Notably in the twentieth century have been the organizations led by Daddy Grace, Father Divine, and Prophet Jones. These movements have several traits in common: (1) charismatic leadership, (2) total submission to their leader, and (3) unyielding discipline. Unfortunately, appearances and performances frequently have taken the place of substance in these movements. The charisma of the leader is sustained by showmanship and dramatic displays. Followers become so devoted to the leader that they would give him (almost always a man) their earthly possessions if he asked. In fact, many have no existence aside from the shadowy glory of the charismatic leader. Total submission is the price the followers pay for what they see as total security. For them the exchange is more than fair, it reflects the benevolence of the charismatic leader. Often the more flamboyant the leader, the more devoted his followers are to him as their special savior.

While these smaller churches are not as prevalent as the Baptists and A.M.E. churches, they do represent the aspirations of a large segment of the black community. Much like these churches are the sub-stratum storefront and shotgun barrel churches that seem to occupy every corner not already occupied by a gasoline station. They are usually headed by a "leader" who believes he is charismatic, frequently he is not more than a distraught preacher who was ousted from a larger church. If this is the case, then his storefront is referred to as a splinter group of a larger church. But even so these secondary churches account for a sizable number of church people and money. This feature of the black Christian community alone could provide considerable support to the coming rise of the spirits.

When the infiltration by young men and women, conscientious cadres, takes place these and other churches will painfully come into the forefront of religious leadership. They will be the innovators, the politically aware partners to Afrocentricity. The church, as a whole, has vacillated on too many issues, wagged its tail too eagerly for the wrong reasons, and lost the trust and confidence of many youthful supporters. They will only return when they are given the choice of a relevant ideology. Deliberate and willful attempts must be made to change these organizations into Afrocentric units. In the next few years, this conscientious cadre will go to church.

They will make of the Black Church what the Ukranians made of their churches, what the Armenians made of theirs, and what the Jews have made of their synagogues: places where children receive cultural and historical training. Such training cannot be left to the schools. Since we have so many churches in the community with buildings going unused on Saturdays, why not Saturday schools?

Clearly the church institutions is the major group force in the black community, outpolling the political parties as well as the civil rights organizations. Yet it has traditionally represented a conservative corpus of opinion and has not fully participated in the emergence of the various enlightenment periods in black history. They have usually started outside the church. Martin L. King's movement was an exception. He was able to captivate most of the Baptists and many members of other churches, primarily because he was a Baptist preacher, his faith was their faith, and as a man of God he combined the best qualities of the charismatic leaders with the passionate rhetoric of the black Baptist to translate grievances into marches and discrimination into sit-ins, walk-ins, and pray-ins. It was the black Baptist civil rights movement. While a few A.M.E. ministers held some secondary posts, the top positions in King's movement were always held by Black Baptist preachers. Notwithstanding its relatively broad appeal, it failed to include the principal leaders of other black denominations. Perhaps Rev. Shuttlesworth, Rev. Abernathy, Rev. Walker, and Rev. Jackson, Rev. Young, and a host of lesser Baptists represented a united front emotionally and theologically that may not have been so with non-Baptists in the chief positions. But this is history, it only serves us as the launching pad from where we make the next ascent. The church, possessing significant power, figures in the Afrocentric resurrection.

Unknown to many worshippers the black church is among our most authentic contact with the gods of our ancestors. The manifestations are present for any interested observer to behold. For we are not speaking here merely on the basis of opinion or hearsay, but on concrete demonstrations. The fact that worshippers have not made the connection between these manifestations and our ancestors is the result of ancestral discontinuity, caused more by the unavailability of proper information regarding Africa than anything else. The church has contributed to this ignorance by obfuscating the discussion of the African past. Indeed, the collective religious experience in the black church harks back to the time when our ancestors called the *loas* and *orishas* with the polymetric beats of the drums. Thus, it should be clear that it is not the church nor its symbols which give power and spirit; it is the spirit of our ancestors found even in the blues and jazz night clubs of our communities. We are a people in tune with our God-force whether in a night club or a church. The feeling is the same; it comes from the same place, it is not merely a church phenomenon and we must cease giving that credit only to the church. The spirit exists whether we experience entertainment or a sermon.

Nevertheless the music and dance of the church may be the essence of our Africanity. What I mean by this is that the panorama of Africa is not merely unfolded but expanded and amplified in the religious drama. More than this, the church services become a collective outpouring of the soul with some people getting more possessed than others but no only really escaping the influence of possession even if it is no more than the slight tapping of the foot. Syncopated pianos and organs and hand-clapping often drive the faithful into ecstasy. The rhythms run to be free, individuals shout and moan, the preacher directs this "mass madness," which is really not madness, by the call and response, and suddenly the whole congregation is praising the Lord. This is truly an African expression, imitated by white evangelicals who first saw African slaves "getting religion." What the Africans were getting, however, was the same ecstatic combinations produced by the polymeters of African music. In the place of drums the African-American substituted hand-clapping, foot-stomping, head-shaking, body-moving rhythm—all in an attempt to drive the self into further possession, by the Lord. While this does not occur in all black churches, it is the general experience of those traditional black churches which have emerged out of the roots of our past. Here the believer who has attends all of the church meetings and listens to all of the preaching and music, land is never possessed is considered abnormal, strange, unusual. For to be captured by the dynamism of the religious experience is to compliment the orchestration of that experience which is one's own work in concert with fellow believers.

Because the black Christian church, in varying degrees, knows this rhythmic catharsis, it is uniquely capable of transmitting knowledge of the past. In fact the church is the most logical institution for the beginning work of instructing the masses concerning African customs, habits, and styles. The various secret societies, or societies of secrets, of Africa mirror the intense emotional quality of the church and because of this fact alone become paradigms for Afrocentric discussion. Quite early in our American sojourn we adapted the internal strivings of our souls, the religious needs and desires, to the western religious experience making a combination with African essence and Christian form. In the centuries since our forefathers and foremothers effected this change we have forgotten why it was done. Nevertheless, most of us still retain the urge to shout whether we are Baptist or not.

Almost naturally, therefore, the church has a split personality, it suffers from Du Bois' dilemma. Its problems are more serious than the "double consciousness" of a single individual (while that is not to be minimized either) because the church is our most pervasive institution. As goes the church so go the church members. The church's peculiar problem appears to be the inability to make up its mind on significant political and social questions. And often when its mind is made up rather than act as a change agent it defends the *status quo*. Hence, as I stated earlier, the black church has been both a catalyst and a dissuader on questions of social and political justice. This is unfortunate in light of the two points already made regarding the church's numerical and historical value. The observations made by Kenneth Clark in *Dark Ghetto* effectively demonstrate the inability of the church to move on social and political matters. The tension between the conservative minded financial supporters and the demands of the social situation frequently put a slipknot around the church's possible idealism. While there is a growing dissatisfaction with the church's commitment to the social, political, and economic plight of its membership, it nevertheless retains the potential for active regeneration.

How do we begin to revamp the church? In other words, how can the church make its best contribution to the rise of the spirits? It is necessary to understand that the church is only secondarily a theological institution, it is primarily a social institution concerned more with fellowship than with dogma. This situation is especially conducive to the role it must play in Afrocentricity. And this fact is confirmed by the church's predominance on the social pages of the various newspapers. So long as this condition holds, and it is certainly not to change in this generation, the resurrection of the church is certain to occur.

What is coming is a cadre of ministers who will drive the church toward revolutionary social and political consciousness. There will be many controversies over strategies as well as objectives, but in the end the innovations of this cadre of ministers will have permanently altered the structure of the black church. They will see themselves in the fighting images of Nat Turner, Henry McNeal Turner, Adam Clayton Powell, and Martin Luther King, Jr. Such a cadre is presently preparing itself in the logics and methods of Afrocentricity. What is different about these young ministers is that they recognize the tremendous social and political power within the black church and they intend to wield that power. Those ministers who formulate clear political and social philosophies based on the African center will completely alter the church's emphasis. A powerful ministerial turnover will effectively entrench the revolutionary cadre of ministers.

Once this occurs, the value of the church to our general revival will become even clearer. The aware ministers represent only the first change awaiting the church. Along with the administrative changes will come new theological directions to support the redirected objectives of the church. Black people have always had some consciousness of God even though this God consciousness was more characterized by social relationships than anything else. Earlier black preachers were usually unconcerned with *immanence, hermeneutical analysis, kerygma,* and *dogmatics.* While the new direction will not mean a concentration on theological dogma, it will mean a reinterpretation of traditional theology. This is why James Cone's liberation theology is prophetic and reflects the application of the black mind to traditional precepts. Cone's interpretations stem from the African-American experience. The work of Albert Cleage is the most obvious example of true transformation of the church. The shrines of the Black Madonna in Detroit, Houston, and Atlanta are on the way to becoming centers of education. Cleage has captured the essence of what a church ought to be in the African-American community. And while the shrines are further along than any other institutions they still are not yet fully Afrocentric. You, liberated and seeking community, can assist the shrines in their total commitment. Many black ministers are responding to this transformation toward a theology with revolutionary meaning.

God must speak out on the subject of black liberation, and the churches must interpret God's answers for the church members. This interpretation must not be merely a re-painting of Jesus to look black; it must be a theology which reflects our history. And as the most authentic respository of our African heritage, the church will meet its most urgent mission. The declaration of a new Afrocentric theology, a doctrine, promulgated by revolutionary preachers who will help alter the church's apolitical and moral stance will create economic, social and political programs to address the present and future needs of Africans in America. Indeed, a new day will have come in the history of the church.

The result of this change will be dramatic. Conversions to political theories and actions will break out on the religious horizon; ministers will preach doctrines based on new symbols. Black madonnas will give way to new symbols arising out of the lives of Isis, Yaa Asantewaa, and Nzingha. This is the minimum requirement for mental resurrection. Then the rituals and liturgies will reflect social dynamism; religion will have come of age. Christianity will be taken out of its white encasement and placed in the ebony wrappings of the people's spirit as a transition to the total stripping to the bone of the church as it is presently constituted in order to be reclothed with the apparatus of an Afrocentric idea.

This black context to the second power is a mirror of the world context. But an interpretation which begins with us merely uses the known bases to move off into the deeper spaces. Already Henry Mitchell and some few other black theologians are seeing the dimensional aspects of black preaching. They are trying to figure out how we say things and what things we say from the pulpits. This is redefinition. Further still, it is interpretation because all genuine redefinition ends in interpretation, and expansion of concepts, and extension of vision. Certainly the results of this change will unfold a drama of immense proportions. Many of the themes are not now clearly seen; yet any phenomenal alteration in the most pervasive institution within the black community means that a new spirit emerges and, Afrocentricity will rise on the sanctification and deification of our history as a way to save ourselves. We are on the edge of a decisive time. And even without complete knowledge of its manifold directions and consequences, one can sufficiently approach the clearing to see that its ideas and concepts will vastly differ from previous forms. It will be an intentional church, meaning to do what it does, actively seeking to affect the state of things, to change minds, to alleviate injustices, and to demonstrate forthright leadership in human affairs. It will be, as it ought to be, the place of God on earth consciously dealing and swinging with everyone but with motifs, symbols, and values from our heritage.

Only when this happens, as it surely will, can we understand James Cone's insistence that religion which is not concerned with black liberation is irrelevant. As victims of whiteness, surrounded by a history of torture, bigotry, and death, we represent the key to freedom—as Nat Turner was free when he chose to defy oppression. There is no freedom without oppression; it destroys oppression, reduces it to nothingness. The church understands this and will inter-realize and amplify that knowledge as it marches into the next generation.

What we must guard against are the charlatans who would use the church for personal gain and who would play Vesey's tattlers to our movements for religious liberation. They must be exposed when they are discovered, and must be measures taken to insure that charlatans will be uncovered regardless to the size and place of the church. Preachers who love to preach because they will be able to ride in Cadillacs and Chryslers must be prevented from assuming leadership roles in the community. Ours is a serious endeavor and there can be no place for religious demagogues who do little for body or spirits. The Afrocentric, vital and dynamic movement, rises every day in a thousand hearts.

Race and Identity

Abdias do Nascimento and Leila Gonzales arise out of the crucible of Brazilian society to speak to the world. In both there is the same humanistic stream found running through the spirits of African people, a deep respect for the sacred, for harmony, for rhythm, for righteousness. While Leila Gonzales sees the resistance movement among Africans in Brazil to be connected to the universal victory of African peoples, she is committed to the Afrocentric rise of the African Brazilian. Nascimento, a revolutionary by birth, challenges the white-accepted science and history of his nation, outlining in great detail the machinations of the Protuguese against African culture.

Nascimento is foremost a dramatist. In many ways he is like a great Mzilikazi treading in deep waters only to find that the waters beckon him to come. And in the history of Afrocentricity it will have to be written that Nascimento more than any other Brazilian of African descent articulated the plight of the Africans in Brazil in our universal language. With the attendant *pathos* and *ethos* necessary for the indelible stamping of truth on the minds Nascimento writes of the false promise, distortions, persecutions, and victories experienced by our people in Brazil. In his European shattering book, *Mixture of Massacre: The Genocide of a People*, he leaves no stump unburned as he marches through the Portuguese treatment of the African. The color codes of Brazil by which Africans were supposed to be whitened so that in the long run there would be neither white nor black but a new Brazilian are shown to be elaborate set-ups for the genocide of black people. In effect, the Brazilian government seeks to have all blacks aspiring to be whites. This would eliminate the Africans. The project has run into difficulty because of the huge numbers of blacks in the society, more than fifty million. Racial "democracy" has meant that the white-skinned people advanced at the expense of the black-skinned ones.

In Brazil as in the United States racism is the principal contradiction, although agitated and aggravated by class because a sort of caste system exists between the colors in Brazil; whereas in America one drop of African blood placed one in a racial caste. Only the Afrocentric analysis of

Nascimento and Gonzales can provide our brothers and sisters in Brazil with direction. If they look to Portugal, they will only find a famine of the soul. Historically derived truths are the only real truths. No greater record of resistance appears in our history than that of the Africans in Brazil who established the first free republic in the Americas. With an Afrocentric analysis one can predict the coming to be of a full protest movement in Brazil which will result in a consciousness of victory based upon Afrocentric connections. Ours is a universal spirit whose imperative will be made evident in every corner of the world, and particularly where our people are mistreated. The Brazilian example is instructive, the provocative intelligence of Nascimento is prophetic.

Marxism

Marxism over-simplifies the significance of our history. The idea that the whole history of the world is merely the record of the struggle of classes dismisses the racist factor in non-homogeneous industrialized nations. Everything is a reflection of economics for Marxism. There is almost no understanding of race and culture. Thus, Marxism does not answer questions which confront people of African descent in societies where Europeans control the economics. Any view that does not recognize culture, race, and state as contributing factors in the debate but only a group of self-interested individuals and classes misses the intractable nature of racism and the essential value of culture. (Asante, 1978).

In some ways Marxism acts on the same Eurocentric base as capitalism because for both life is economics, not culture. The class-warrior attitude dominates the thinking of Marxists and capitalists. It is a war of class against class, group against group, and individual against individual. Neither system finds fault with the destruction of one's economic enemy so long as criminal laws are not violated. One may absolutely wipe out the economic competition in the capitalist system and be applauded. Marxism, on the other hand, allows open warfare on the bourgois class.

Operating on the European values of confrontation developed from the adventures of Europeans during the terrible White Ages, both of these systems believe in utter destruction of aliens. This, of course, is contradictory to the Afrocentric value which respects difference and applauds pluralism. Strangers exist in that they have not been known. They bring good fortune and therefore are welcomed. In economics, therefore, Marxism's base is antithetical to the African concept of society. Life for the Afrocentric person is organic, harmonious, and cultural because it is integrated with African history. However, the Marxist view of life is as competitive as that of the capitalist, since both are rooted in Eurocentric materialism. Thus, the competitor of the working class is the bourgeoisie and the victory of the working class is the principal aim of world history, such confrontational politics seems to inhere in the Eurocentric view.

Marxism's Eurocentric foundation makes it antagonistic to our worldview; its confrontational nature does not provide the spiritual satisfaction we have found in our history of harmony. This history of harmony, stemming from a strong sense of God-consciousness in nature and each other, is denied by European materialism which views harmony as a lack of progress. Progress, in a Eurocentric manner, grows out of conflict, a sort of dialectic of forces. For us, life is culture, spirit, and harmony. Therefore, we accept no dictatorship of any kind. The Afrocentric denounces a dictatorship of the proletariat as well as that of the bourgoisie. And at any rate once a classless society exists, to whom will the dictatorship of the proletariat dictate? Certainly not Africans! We can never allow the expropriators to expropriate our spirit, our culture or our lives. Marxism explains European history from a Eurocentric view; it does not explain African culture from an Afrocentric view. It is in fact the ultimate example of European rationalism (Moore, 1972).

Science

The religion of science, with its rituals, priesthood, orthodoxy, apostates, liturgy, and converts, it is the dominant outlook of the western world. It is a religion based upon the search for absolute knowledge of phenomena, it therefore becomes materialistic. When we understand this, we will have a sharper understanding of the European mind. Darwin, Marx, Freud laid a foundation for western science. They were the beneficiaries of Descartes and Leibniz and Newton. They turned their intellectual energies to discreet and not-so-discreet phenomena rather than to ultimate realities and truths. Theirs was a world of specific phenomena, not a world of wholes. According to this religion of science, a disputant is considered a heretic and to be "unscientific" is to engage in heresy.

This religion of science sees everything as profane, nothing is sacred except man. With this view of the world European man often assumes himself to be a god. The scholar becomes the priest, the assistant professor the altar-boy, and Newton, Darwin, and Freud are made saints to be worshipped.

The Afrocentric perspective upholds the significance of science; indeed in the sense that it is based upon history and heritage; Afrocentricity is itself a science. Western science, with its notions of knowledge of phenomena for the sake of knowledge and its emphasis on technique and efficiency is not deep enough for our humanistic and spiritual viewpoint. Therefore its limitations are clearly revealed in our history. As Karenga has said, we are not into spookism. We are, however, most definitely into African *personalism* energizing every aspect of nature. Where the West is said to favor materialism and the East, meaning largely India, is said to favor spiritualism, Africa combines the material and spiritual. *Personalism* invades the material as well as the spiritual. For us, therefore, the trees and the mountains have always possessed essences. We do not have to make absolute distinctions between mind and matter, form and substance, ourselves and the world. The self is the center of the world, animating it, and making it living and personal. Neither materiality nor spirituality are illusory. This is why the idea in western science of progress is troubling. Progess, for the West, is not more knowledge but more technique. How to do it faster, smoother, longer, louder, and with greater exploitation becomes the pass key to a techno-scientific future. Progress, in an Afrocentric manner, is related to the development of human personality because we are the source of life for the material and the spiritual; when we become more conscious of ourselves we shall be advanced and will make progress.

The bankruptcy of western technics is clear for all to see. Those who participate in Western technics seek technical solutions to everything. It is again the strong inherent desire in European man growing out of the nomadic, hunting context of Europe that makes him seek conquest of nature. Accordingly, the land was harsh and yielded little food, so machinery would rid the world of poverty. European tribes warred against each other, so inventions would be created so terrible that wars would be outmoded. Men die, so all disease would be conquered eliminating the pathology that caused death, and so forth. Scientific god-fathers would control everything and everyone and science would remain supreme.

Increasingly the western world will be turned back to the original ideas of Africa. Already with systems thinking, the idea of entropy, probability in statistics, and the admission that much phenomena are subjective concepts, the western outlook rises toward the Afrocentric view. For example, while some western "scientists" used to believe in the reality of "atom," "neutron," "energy," and "gravity," they now admit that these are merely descriptive concepts to help explain the metaphysics that otherwise cannot be explained. We know that the more you study any of these concepts the closer to spirituality you will come. The quarks now considered the smallest units of the atom cannot be measured. Let us consider the size of the atom—in diameter it is a ten-millionth of a millimeter. If you took the mass of a sodium atom and compared it to one gram of water, the sodium atom would be about the size of a small book to the size of the earth. Electrons are smaller still and quarks are far smaller. Even the material units of western science dissolve into the Afrocentric understanding of the unity of man and nature. We cannot be antagonistic to nature and the abnormality as manifest in the European's desire to defy nature is antithetical to our perspective.

Science in the West has given way to a more entrenched technics. While science parades as a mental discipline, technics shows us no such drama. We are left believing that technique is the source of everything the West attempts, there is no soul, no feeling, no emotion, only technique. It is a politics of the manipulation of things and substances as opposed to human significance. How many nuclear reactors are possible in one state? Can this mountain be moved? What are the possibilities of building a bigger bomb? Can we ascertain the results of energy loss in a certain place? How do we dispossess the Africans to steal their land and have them believe we are doing them a favor? Technics is its own value.

The absolute repudiation of techniques for its own sake is a cardinal value of Afrocentricity. We do not understand art, dance, scholarship, or music which is merely technique. As people who place a high value on expressiveness from within, radiance in art, music, scholarship, and dance, we find it impossible to accept the clean, sharp lines of technics as representative of the best in the human race. Indeed our view is that beauty inheres in human beings and can be revealed through sincerity and goodwill. Dance is not only the technique; music is not merely technique. Thus, we rise above the decadence of western science and technics to the *orisha* of Afrocentricity.

Aesthetics

All aesthetics find their sources in resemblance (Welsh, 1979). When you say that you like something or do not like something, you are speaking on the basis of an idea in your mind about what resembles you. This is more than physical resemblance, it is spiritual, emotional, and intellectual resemblance as well. In most instances, it reflects the idealized versions of ourselves. Thus, the beautiful person is not necessarily a look-alike of me but one who possesses the qualities I most admire. Only by understanding this relationship between aesthetics and ourselves can we truly understand and appreciate Afrocentricity. It is an aesthetics which stems from the pure relationship of our thoughts and our total selves. The person who does not enjoy the orator because his voice is rhythmic is giving us an idea about his own voice—perhaps monotony is his ideal. The person who looks at dancers and says, "I cannot stand to watch them, they are like rubber bands," is also speaking from his own still ideal of what a dancer should be.

An Afrocentric aesthetic will not allow the loss of our culture, in fact, it augments the culture by adding new symbols to the aesthetic. Literature, dance, art, and theater are revolutionized because they not only speak to us or of us but *from* us. In essence, the smart Harlem Renaissance poets were speaking of us to others. What we are seeing in Njia poets and writers is a new *Nia*, namely, to speak from our center for our people. This aesthetic is neither narrow nor limiting as some critics have stated. They misconstrue not only the nature of Afrocentricity but also of art. All art is culture bound; to deny the Afrocentrist a cultural base by claiming that Afrocentricity is narrow mirrors one of the continuing problems with white-washed brains.

Artists in every society seek to express in their works what is natural to them. Why should the Afrocentrist using the natural concerns of his/her culture be considered provincial? For us, the only provincial art is that which has no function for the people. No aesthetic is as broad for the Afrocentric person as Afrocentric aesthetics. It allows fantasy, relief, drama, irony, humor, conflict, history, and imagination. A committed and functional art advances the people and enhances the culture. Otherwise, it is the shallow commercial art, in the sense of individual capitalist exploitation of self, which occurs. Apart from its ultimate futility, it is contradictory to artistic history. Ice skating, ballet, and opera are from a Eurocentric context for Eurocentric audiences to be critically assessed by Eurocentric judges. This is as it should be. It does not mean that Africans and Asians cannot perform those arts; obviously they perform them as well sometimes as the Europeans. However, the performance must be evaluated according to criteria developed from a European setting. If an African wants to compete in ballet, she must understand that the criteria are not universally derived but culturally specific. She must submit to the rigors of the European view of what ballet is and what it is not. There is no mystery in this except when an African or European insists that Afrocentricity is narrow. The truth is that they are so enraptured by Eurocentric thought that they cannot see the entrapment. They do not understand that there are other ways to think, to see, to dance, to sing, to view reality.

The predicament of our arts would be different if our artists practiced Afrocentricity. Such a development would add even more lustre to the power of our creative ethos as we control the dissemination, presentation and interpretation of our art.

Form, feeling, and time (rhythm) are the key criteria in discussing the aesthetic for black people. The form, feeling, and rhythm must come out of our cultural consciousness or memory. Black people, internationally, can draw upon a collective bank that houses images, symbols, references, and resources based upon history and mythology. The court dances of every ethnic group in Africa would embody a particular behavior on the part of royalty and the subject. This dance would become part of the race memory and the aesthetic would support all artistic expressions that would relate to the particular aspect. Much like the ballets of today and the still visible court dances and attitudes of Louis XIV, it is the Eurocentric aesthetic that makes these images and symbols habit for artists before the act of expression begins. We must be mindful that art is expression of impressions, not expression of expression. Therefore, it is a responsible consideration to rely upon a conscious impression. In the art of Africans and African-Americans, it is the conscious expression of that impression and experience, whether individual or collective, that drives our aesthetic.

Richard Wright insists that "tradition is no longer a guide" in determining a black aesthetic. It is that particular and elitist form of ignorance that has made tradition, culture, and mythology dirty words for the aspiring black artist. Tradition is, of course, history, customs, and rituals. Tradition changes; it is not static, but rather a perspective that is controlled by the viewers. We need not make tradition out to be an obstacle but rather a necessary link between an individual and his particular mode of expression as well as his means of expression. Another myth that has hurt in the creation of a viable functional aesthetic is that African-Americans were bereft of their African heritage. That was the intention, and results from a Eurocentric point of view. What happened from the Afrocentric point of view was that overt activity manifesting African heritage was denied but the spirit, intuitive, metaphysical and impressions were still very much African and consequently, the tradition changed with these "new" eyes of the viewer.

The Afrocentric aesthetic would not beg the questions of freedom, it would create and establish freedom and identify its own audiences. The aesthetic itself would be self-reliant and the artist would address herself to the collective will of the people. Our folklore also is manifestation of our culture. Do not allow others to divorce our brilliant folklore from our legacy. We must not give ourselves "folklore" in the pejorative sense of European usage and deny ourselves our culture, nor must we contribute to the false idea that folklore and culture are separate. Folklore emanates from culture. We have a victorious folklore, check it out.

Chapter 4
The Bases of Action

Tactics and Strategies

Frederick Douglass once said that the African had to speak with the front of his head rather than the back in order to achieve true victory. What he meant was that our objective had to remain constant while we changed means. All our philosophers have understood the distinction between tactics and strategy. A profound sense of the collective imperative carries us toward our strategy. In the process of achieving social, political, and economic victory over the negatives within us, we shall arrive at our objective through various tactics.

A strategy is a long-term plan for achieving an objective while tactics are the science of arranging and managing the details of human behavior. Afrocentricity does not negate strategies nor tactics; it recognizes their individual places in the overall thrust toward victory. In this respect, it may be tactically wise to perform some task, make some pledge, or carry out some action. This is permissible so long as the profound objective remains the overall strategy for achieving the objective.

When our tactics become the objective, we fall victims to self-deception. Many of our thinkers have warned us of the danger of this view. There can be but one true objective for us in the contemporary era; to reconstruct our lives on an Afrocentric base. Such a strategic objective finds its place in all areas of life. We must study African contact with Europe in search of the pathology which drives Europeans toward avarice and exploitation in relationship to others. Strategy means that the Afrocentrist seeks to uncover all falsehoods, to expose fake issues, to demonstrate the overpowering effect of committed will in changing behaviors.

Most of the projects and schemes promulgated by community organizations and civil rights groups lack strategy, although they possess innumerable tactics for their operations. Some seek to teach our children how to excel. Some seek to get us on buses and into integrated schools; and some seek to get us jobs or better jobs. The question is, what is the objective? Why should we excel, be integrated, or work? There is no reason for any of these tactics unless they work toward the profound Afrocentric objective. So we develop a mathematics or verbal whiz, for what? So we integrate, and then what? So we get all kinds of high-paying jobs, and what happens? Do we lose our souls to gain whitening? I am opposed to all programs to excel which do not have an Afrocentric base. I reject, as all Afrocentrists must, blind allegiance to integrated lifestyles which do not allow Afrocentric living. I must object to job programs which do not teach values and purpose to the would-be workers. Indeed, these types of projects are tactics which cannot alleviate the African's burden. Consequently, Afrocentrists are in the best position to call for reconstruction of our values since they are keenly aware of the dangers which still cloud our reconstructive paths.

Deviations

Political, social, and cultural activities must be scrutinized constantly. *Deviations are intentional or unintentional misapplications of symbols and images which subvert the collective consciousness of our people.* The Afrocentrist must challenge the symbolic ideas of the person who does not consistently apply the truth of Afrocentricity. To demonstrate his ability to recite the names of the kings of England and not know Menes, Djoser, Sneferu, Pepi, Akhenaten, Rameses, Piankhy, or Shabaka is a deviation. To learn the lineage of David and not know the principal kings of Benin— Igodo, Ere, Akhuankhuan, Owodo, Evian, Eweka, Esigie, Obanosa, and Adolo is to deviate. Knowledge in its active state of information becomes the conscious key to power. That is why all behavior must be analyzed for its Afrocentric base.

To say that "such and such program on television is a good program" means that you have made an Afrocentric analysis. Sometimes a brother would say "the program on King Edward of England was fantastic!" If the brother makes that statement from an Afrocentric perspective, that is, he asks if it is in the best interest of Afrocentricity? then it becomes a conscious statement. If not, then he misunderstands the contextual nature of good and evil. Good is contextual; so is evil. Therefore, one must know precisely what he is talking about when he argues that something is good which is not from an Afrocentric perspective. One could mean that when I looked at the television program I saw how we could reconstruct the symbolic images of Martin Delaney, Shabaka, Eweka, Marcus Garvey, or Edward Blyden. Afrocentric analysis applies to everything. The boldness with which you practice it will affect the geometric expansion of the collective conscious will.

When you fly in an airplane and see the designs of the cabins, think how you would design it Afrocentrically. When you build an automobile, think how your engineering can be more Afrocentric. When you have to write a paper, think how it can be made more Afrocentric. When you plant seeds, think how the ancestors can give you that power. When you organize politically, do it in the best interest of African people. Whatever is in our best interest is always in the best interest of all people. You are the miracle of the way.

Practice the logic of Afrocentricity which originates in the Kemetic texts. That is, analyze according to questions; do not be befuddled by your own traditions. Understand that to break concepts down into concrete realities is a very Afrocentric analytical procedure. When you are asked a question, assume that the answer can be broken down into concrete parts. If someone asks you, "What time is it?" your response can be direct, "It is nation time" or "It is 8 o'clock?" Or your response may be analytical. "Do you mean politically, socially, culturally, or economically?" You do this not to demonstrate how intelligent you are because that is a given; you do it to teach the querist how to analyze.

The logic of Afrocentricity is immutable, non-contradictory, and consolidating. It is immutable because it is based on the reality of yourself; you know yourself first. If you use a logic outside of yourself, you know that it is artificial and alien. Only the logic, symbolic relationships, derived from your center can create the necessary power for reconstruction. It is non-contradictory because it takes the symbols created from your center and connects them to symbols created by other people in order to advance the collective conscious imperative. Our imperative is based upon the ever-present reality of ourselves. Act on the basis of Afrocentricity and you will consolidate your own spiritual powers as well as join the symbolic universe of our cognitive wills. Deviations lead to the fog which surrounds those who wander from their centers. All people have a perspective which stems from their centers.

Afrocentricity has its own Njia based upon historically correct perceptions of reality. All such perceptions contribute to the profound Njia upon which we must stand. Our creators sometimes unfortunately mix realities. Thus, we have those writers who write passages such as:

The sun was setting. *Raymond* could feel the cold wind. His face *flushed* and he called to *Helen* to see if the snow was falling. It was. And he thought it was so *pure* and *righteous*.

While Afrocentricity does not deny anyone the right to create, it seeks to direct the creation in a positive manner. Every creation adds to reality. In fact, there is no reality apart from creation. I know that what our writers choose, what our artists choose, what our choreographers choose become someone's reality. The warped version of their own reality may be fastened onto future generations by our lack of vigilance. Skill in Afrocentric creativity takes *training* and *commitment*. Training provides the creators with the limits and commitment allows the creators to perfect her/his skill in practice.

The list of deviations is finite which means that we can truly know everything if we perfect ourselves by practice. Some of the more obvious deviations are in the literary area.

When the European says, "this city is like a jungle" understand that he is speaking from his own center. To him "jungle" is synonymous with violence, struggle, each person ready to attack the other and anarchy. But consider "jungle" realistically and you will immediately see that Afrocentricity gives a different perspective. Linguistically, the word jungle is derived from the Sanskrit "jangala" meaning "desert." It was later used to mean primitive and savage and then applied to the African rain forest. In actuality the idea of impenetrable forest as jungle is foreign to most of Africa since it is the Asian and South American rain forests which have the characteristic of tangled bush and vines. At any rate, the forest is not a place of violence or anarchy. Some great cities and villages are surrounded by forest. The idea conjured by a Eurocentric view of jungle is one which derives from their encounter with the West African rain forest. Swamps, crocodiles, and malaria impressed forever a scary feeling about the forest. So that is why when they say it is a jungle I know they mean the *steppes*. In my view of reality, the rain forest protected me from them; the *steppes* where they fought each other with vengeance, every ethnic group out to annihilate every other one is violent; so when I think of some place that is violent, antagonistic and anarchistic, I say "man, it is like the steppes."

"He is a Judas" is another such deviation. My history teaches me that when a person reveals private information entrusted to him he is a 'Vesey's tattler." Every reality that needs to be addressed is a reality within our historical framework. The people who told on Vesey were worse than

Judas. Judas betrayed one man; they betrayed a whole people. It is necessary that we watch our commitment lest we be adversely recorded in our history. What will be say about writers, researchers, and artists whose orientations are toward Europe? Listen, it is already being said. Can you hear the thunder?

"What kind of salad dressing do you prefer?" This question heard thousands of times in American and European culinary establishments elicits replies like "French," "Russian," or "Italian." We are asked to participate subconsciously in the drama of Europe. Since the first edition of *Afrocentricity: The Theory of Social Change* we now have sauces and dressings with names like Ghanaian, Nigerian, Senegalese and Tanzanian. The idea is that the Afrocentrist refuses to be inundated by a symbolic reality which denies her existence. We must reconstruct on the basis of commitment not reaction. That is why, perhaps, we have yet to perfect our mark here. As these words appear on this page, the collective imperative will of our people will change this situation. Now we must act.

Every time an African achieves heroic stature in defense of our people, someone labels her or him a Moses. Harriet Tubman was called the "Moses of her people." Touissaint L'Ouverture was the "Moses of the West Indies" and Marcus Garvey was "the Black Moses." Let us refuse to participate in such nonsense. Harriet, Touissaint, and Marcus are unique in their own right. No comparison with Moses is necessary or meaningful. This genre of derivation occurs in many ways like the "Black Picasso," "The Black Newton," "The Black Maria Callas," etc. A book by an African American carried the title *The Black Apollo of Science* when, if anything, the origin of European philosophy and creative thought came from Africans. George James makes this point in his book, *Stolen Legacy* (1976),

To say that you are going to the continent must mean you are going to Africa. It is the home of the human race and the origin of civilization. When Africans speak like Europeans about the continent of Europe, it is puzzling. The European who says "I have just come from the continent" will find me asking, "What were you doing in Africa?" To me it is the center from which I interpret. When someone says "middle ages" you must ask, whose middle ages? When they say "classical" you must ask, whose classical? Only in this way can you prevent Eurocentrism from imposing itself as universal. This is its most poignant difference with Afrocentricity. While Eurocentrism imposes itself as universal; Afrocentricity demonstrates that it is only one way to view the world. The fact that people educated by westerners know Marco Polo but not always Ibn Battuta is a function of Eurocentric imposition in education. A word like *stoic* comes out of Greek history; *Spartan* comes out of the same general history. I say instead Zulu and

Masai. No army was ever as disciplined as Chaka's Army who ruled without horses over a territory that stretched for thousands of miles! And the Spartans never had anything on the Masai or Nubians.

The Afrocentric vocabulary does not include the use of the word minority because the identity of the people included in one's meaning is necessary. Therefore, we say African-Americans, Puerto Ricans, Columbians, Cubans, etc. We cannot continue to use this ambiguous term created by a European to designate non-Europeans.

Expand upon this list. Go over it with each other and add to it in discussion, print, and media. Make your reality known in victory. Imagination literally means to *image-a-nation*. You must do this through study and reconstruction.

Commitment to Greatness

Chancellor Williams is correct to understand the relatedness of nutrition and development of a national concept. Starving people cannot lead a nation or develop an ideology. All ideologies have been articulated by inspired individuals who have adequate access to food sources. Williams must be properly understood in *The Destruction of Black Civilization* when he says that the lack of food leads to genocide, mental retardation, sluggishness, mental fatigue, and poor sense of security. Indeed, people must be famine free and unified. People must maintain a strong army, be in control of their land and its resources, and have a sense of equal justice for all in order to administer the nation. Although Williams' analysis is consistent with the best Afrocentric thought, it should be noted the black civilization was not destroyed as his title maintains but distorted, maimed, and sidetracked. The vigor of African civilization resisted all attempts at destruction. Nevertheless, Williams is one of our most brilliant historical thinkers because he captured the essence of our past and interpreted it for the future.

In another regard, among the concepts derived from Williams, Jackson, and Ben-Joachannan is the power of a committed few (Jackson, 1970). The national idea, galvanized by Afrocentricity, is always in the mind of a relatively small group of people. In the course of its fulfillment, the national idea will act in all directions of thought and action as it becomes ever-present. Indeed, a rumble or street fight may be just as important to the expression of a national idea as a poem; a community center as important as a *njia*; a gun as important as a painting. They are all cultural expressions of the people's mode and manner of doing things. This is why Karenga's creative motif is a powerful concept of Afrocentricity. It defines the nature of the expression. I recently saw an exhibit of contemporary Japanese art;

it *looked* like Japanese art. The motif was clear; it was not Persian or Italian or Russian or British or Akan. One knew immediately that it reflected the Japanese art. Well, that is precisely what occurs when the committed few begin to express Afrocentric modes and manners in everything from argument to building a museum.

Each of us in our own way contributes to the maintenance of the national idea by our receptivity to Afrocentricity, which is actually a receptivity to our own center. To those who are not receptive to Afrocentricity, all things become grotesque. They see African-American Studies as an embarrassment to their Eurocentric comfort, African history becomes glorified tales of greatness, Afrocentricity itself becomes racism, and political action becomes unnecessary. Such people should be viewed as reactionary to the national idea. In the debate over race and progress, the present era has seen the emergence of several champions of the Eurocentric perspective. Their inability to see their own unreality suggests the most telling results of their "mentacide'" which BobbyWright defines as the killing of the mind.

It is a mistake to assume that the ideas of black conservatives are innovative. They are voicing the same arguments as white reactionaries and racists of the middle of the nineteenth century. What is new is that there are blacks who are so thoroughly educated in the American system of racism that they have become racist against themselves. These anti-black blacks or the "unblack blacks" who cannot see from within but see other "blacks" as objects from without are marginal.

This stage in the exploitation of African-Americans represents the most violent form of capitalist rationalism to date. Black conservatives grow from a sense of historical discontinuity, inadequate or incomplete consciousness of their people's achievements, and a bitter, almost obscene fear of being African. Both Fanon and Malcolm understood this as the most successful type of the European domination of the victim, when the victim takes the arguments of his oppressor and re-states them as if they are new. Of course, they are given high profile by the white conservatives who created them.

An objective analysis of the facts demonstrated that the general condition of Africans in American society relate to the previous condition of white enslavement of Africans. But black super conservatives negate history because they refuse to accept the source of their problem. Their lack of historical consciousness underscores their inability to approach a problem scientifically. It is like a medical researcher trying to find the cure for a disease. In order to do so, she must first find the cause, that is, the source of the disease. You can more adequately prescribe therapy once you know with what you are dealing. The black super conservatives, like their white counterparts, do not have a grasp of history. This myopia is a sort of selective discontinuity which leads to a disregard for the truth.

The idea that we are America's historical victims is certainly a sound basis for political and economic claims as the African-American Reparations Committee has claimed. Wrongly, the super conservatives view these claims as existing outside of any present interest. The fact of the matter is that America cannot dismiss the political, economic, and psychological set-backs of the 250 years of involuntary servitude without compensation. The people who suffered that collective oppression still carry the memory, the damage, and the legacy. Yet, having said this let me also emphasize that we have surmounted incredible odds since 1865. While these black conservative aesthetes may appease whites when they say that African-American history should not be used as a "moral bludgeon," they demonstrate once again their lack of historical reference to any progress made by Africans in America.

One black conservative contends that our enslavement has little to do with sociological or historical causation. They think that the main effect in evoking the slave experience is moral in that it establishes white culpability. This is only half true. It does not establish white culpability; history does. That is like saying that raising the issue of the holocaust establishes Nazi culpability. That is definitely true but beyond that, sociology, history, psychology, culture, and economics are fundamentally tied to the slave experience. I mean when the African-American person evokes slavery, it is not to put the white person down for his culpability—that is a fact—but rather to see the fuller view which includes the victory over oppression, the creative genius of the high songs, the survival of purpose, the memory of Africa, the union of the ancestors, and the economic plight of Africans here and now, the destruction of cosmologies, the loss of our languages, and the forced separations.

What does the history of white oppression have to do with this? Everything. The continuation of this legacy in a Forsyth County, Mobile, or Howard Beach, or Chicago has much to do with social, cultural, and historical realities. As such, separation of these realities from the moral issue is futile. Not even for the sake of argument should these super black conservatives have spoken of the moral issue as separate from the historical or social. It is a cute intellectual exercise but it has no basis in reality.

The black super conservative normally claims that black political leaders do not deal with personal inadequacies of blacks but rather attribute those inadequacies to the "system." In fact, Glenn Loury claims that leaders of civil rights groups dismiss black shortcomings. He is, of course, mistaken in his analysis and commentary since black political leaders and civil rights spokespersons have dealt with both, so-called "personal inadequacies" and system inadequacies. The problem is that the black super conservatives refuse to see that the system dictates much of what occurs to an individual. The system is not merely the bureaus of government but the racist domination that drives many of the agents of those bureaus which represents the legacy of the white enslavement of blacks. This is precisely the habit, the behavior, the attitude that the individual African-American has fought in order to achieve the remarkable degree of dignity possessed by this heroic people.

Perhaps one of the most self-serving statements appeared in an article in *Public Interest* (1986) where the black conservative Glenn Loury said: "The acknowledgement by blacks of the possibility, within the American constitutional order, of individual success ... comes to be seen as a betrayal of the black poor." Again this is nonsense taken to an extreme level. What must be discussed is not "individual success" but what is *success*. The examples of economic, scientific, political, literary, artistic success are legend within the black community. I know of no one who has even talked about, leave alone, written about, such "success" as being a "betrayal of the black poor." Like white reactionaries, racists, and conservatives, black super conservatives suggest that too much of us made of racism. But the facts of the society speak for themselves:

Such people become the enemies of the national idea, sowing discord whenever they can, disrupting the building of consciousness, scoffing at our achievements, and fraternizing for favor with the historical antagonists of Afrocentricity. Fortunately, we recognize them as intellectual lackeys who have little honor among the people. They talk big and do nothing. When our visionaries arise, they call them megalo-maniacs and ego-maniacs, hoping to crush the vision by labeling the visionary. When the chance affords, these lackeys flog and torture our people like Emmett Till, but them like Chaney, and kick the dead bodies in the midst of the crowds. Such reactionaries parade the grounds of academic institutions, march in private and public service, and hate every minute of work for the people. Needless to say, their work is only for the enemy; they are selfish people who owe no allegiance to truth or justice.

Afrocentricity demands a commitment to greatness based upon the true historical character of the people. Knowing full well that the only road to happiness and harmony is excellence in everything. Our path to that road is set out for each of us by the ancestors. Gainsayers who know no turns but to the right will always try to deny our commitment inasmuch as they deny that commitment in themselves. If it becomes necessary in the name of the people to dig trenches, you must dig the best and most perfect trenches possible. This is the commitment to greatness. It is not a small commitment. During the exile of Karenga, he vowed that the only way for the people to survive the crisis of value was to renew the commitment to greatness. It is precisely as understood by Fanon, Walter Rodney, Tichaona Freedom, and Malcolm X. The measure of our movement for victory is in ourselves, and is written in how we perform the tasks set before us. You cannot say that you are Afrocentric or that you believe in *Njia* and not work for perfection in every aspect of your behavior. It is natural that you should be perfect. We do not assume that "gittin' it together" continues beyond adolescence. Our aim is the powerful reawakening of the spirit that launched Abubakari's two hundred ships, that wrote the *Book of the Coming Forth by Day and the Going Forth by Night*, that erected the pyramids, that built Zimbabwe, and that gave the world the knowledge of the human spirits. A committed few can bring about the refreshing and beautiful spirit of the beginning again and again.

Seizing the Time

Africans are at the center of American history, arriving before the pilgrims, we existed before the American nation. A succession of spokespersons, fro the 18th Century, have understood as much and have been able to capitalize on this centrality. Whether it was Booker T. Washington imploring whites at the Atlanta Exposition of 1895 to "cast down your buckets where you are" or the early Black Panthers and Vernon Jordan of the Urban League making their separate proposals for coalitions with various groups of whites, we have known this truth and have interpreted it as the interweaving of history in the beautiful but troubled land for nearly four hundred years. It is now time for us to activate our collective will to peace and consciousness.

During slavery our fathers and mothers perfected their predictions of white behavior they began to tell only what was acceptable and thus concealed their true beliefs, impressions, and ideas behind masks. It was better, in a survival sense, to tell whites what they wanted to hear and continue to live than to tell unpleasant facts and be "sold down the river." Knowing the Europeans prejudice against Africans, our fathers were cognizant of the inconsistencies of white proclamations.

Politics and economics constitute the decisive sectors of black-white confrontation in the rising of our spirits. Undoubtedly other areas will be affected. But the critical juncture in our path to an unprecedented era of productivity will be the crossroads of economic and political actions.

The next age will be a political age. So the reactions of whites will be political and pragmatic. Regardless of the intervening crises of spirit, whether they be in international politics or spiritual values, the essential European mode of response will be practical. The conservative drive to protect what they will appear to be losing, that is, a dominant role in world politics will force Europeans to respond practically. In fact, the loss if European dominance will be made a reality by numerous contending and allying forces. These forces include the rise of our spirits in the United States, the coming to early consciousness in Brazil, the economic strength and flexibility of Japan, the tightening of internal control over oil production by the African and Arab states, the establishment of a Palestinian state, the hegemony of the Peoples Republic of China over Asia, the transfer of petro-dollars to OPEC, the completion of the Pan-African union among African states, and the further decline of Europe, particularly Britain and France, whose wealth and political clout were built upon external holdings. With these ominous signs, historical certainties, made so by the ever progression of contemporary forces and the sureness of change, and barring nuclear madness which would make everything absurd, white Americans, the preeminent children of Europe, will find pragmatism not merely a philosophical tenet, to be accepted or rejected, but a consummate necessity for survival.

Thus, in politics and economics, new arrangements will have to be made, new pledges taken, and different promises given, for example, it is conceivable that Europeans witnessing the birth of a collective Afrocentricity, not realized since ancient time, will reinterpret political concepts and principles to assure as much as possible the cooperation of the races. But you see, race is neither a biological or anthropological fact, it is a political concept. Its origin like that of nations and states is rooted in the will to command power over other people, and power is predicated upon distinctions and differences. The exacerbation of these differences was at first a political work, only secondarily was it an anthropological trick. That is precisely why anthropology is also the most political of the social sciences. One does not discover even in political science the underlying premises of anthropology. Much more than political science anthropology is a European discipline. In its inception and later in its conspiracies with sociology, it attempted to define the rest of the world in relationship to the European world.

Classification schemes created *Negroid, Mongoloid,* and *Caucasoid* races. Definitions, emerging from the Caucasoid perspective with little claim to objectivity (which is a creation of the same western minds), abounded. Among the political tactics was the comparative definition used in the nineteenth century by European writers who wrote statements like "as compared to the Caucasoid race, the Negroid race has thick lips, flat noses, kinky hair, etc."; but it is a game that can be played by any group interested in political and economic exploitation of other people. Had Afrocentric perspectives been applied, the definition would have been "as compared to blacks, whites have undeveloped lips, pointed noses, limp hair, etc." Anthropological terms forced upon us a concept of race that ultimately legitimized oppression, murder, and genocide. Of course, I cannot say the Malinowski, Levy-Bruhl, and others intentionally created these mental atrocities, but they provided the basic European rationale for racial differences. If you figured that someone was your enemy because his eyes looked differently, now you were able to add a qualitative dimension to your judgment and the anthropologists gave a European perspective to a question which had social and political implications.

The practical end of all of this anthropological inquiry is the presence of ethno-this and ethno-that to once again indicate European dominance. Thus, ethno-rhetoric, ethno-musicology, ethno-science and even ethnography are meant to show the other, to study the other as other and, in fact, inferior. In other words, what Africans create becomes ethno-music not real music and so forth.

What does this mean for the Euro-American response to the rise of our spirits? It is simply this, there will be a positive response to the new era because Afrocentricity will reinterpret history and give whites a new way out of their collective dilemma which results from the gathering intellectual and economic forces. The political concept of race will have to be redefined and then dismissed as an obfuscation of the power relationships which in fact hold sway in this country.

Contemporary African biologists talk about gene pools, genotypes, and phenotypes, ideas which make some sense scientifically. On the other hand, the concept "race" must be dealt with in order to dispense with political nonsense. The political concept "race" will be reinterpreted by Afro-Americans because it has no biological or anthropological basis. In the United States the concept of race reached more limits than any place except Brazil or Azania (South Africa). In the United States, eighteenth and nineteenth century legislatures wrestled with the problem of codifying a meaningless concept and many settled on "any trace of African blood," "any parent, grandparent, or great-grandparent who was an African," etc. Such schemes which were designed to "keep the white race pure" included keeping white women out of bed with black men because offsprings of such unions could only be black. Booker T. Washington aptly noted during one of his swings through the South that "African blood is pretty powerful, just one drop and you are counted on my side." While his white audience roared wild laughter, the point was sharply made that the whole idea of race purity as a concept to be defended is rather absurb.

Strange and weird exchanges occur in such an atmosphere. Whites might even brag, "I'm one fourth Cherokee," because it's considered a bit exotic to be part Indian, after all they don't really constitute any kind of threat; the whites nearly eliminated them. But have you ever heard anyone defined as white say, "I'm one fourth African?" You see, we constitute a potential threat. And quite frankly in those regions of the United States, like the Dakotas, Minnesota, North Carolina, and portions of the Southwest, to claim Indian ancestry is still not considered exotic because in those areas race and group definitions are still political.

What then are the directions of the black reinterpretation? We must first de-policize race as a concept. There are two steps to this de-politicalization: *dismantling* and *restructuring*. Race can only lose its political potency by attacking the white social sciences that persist in creating myths to further enhance the idea of racial purity and superiority. The periodic rebirth of mad white social scientists who claim to bind the definitive case for white superiority is a direct outgrowth of all the mania and phobia created by the political concept of race. Once we dispense with the artificialities of "race" as a political concept we will have won one of the battles to reorder the social questions. Indeed our people have always understood "enia dudu," "watu weusi," "baiki mutane," and "meedidzee" as social realities.

Restructuring does not mean the setting up of race again as a concept but rather the reorganization of the whole identity question in the United States. For each nation the process of identity is different. Brazil, for example, recognized Afro-Brazilians and Luzo-Brazilians; Nigeria recognizes over two hundred ethnic groups; the Soviet Union over one hundred; the Japanese Islands less than five ethnic groups, etc. In the United States most of the people originally came from some place else. The Navajo, Apache, Creek, Choctaw, and numerous other ethnic and linguistic groups were in America when the first people from Africa and Europe arrived. In some respects it should be easy to reorganize indentity labels which would not be reflective of politics but of national or continental origin; in other respects it will be difficult and trying. For example, people identified as Jews often see themselves in both an ethnic and religious sense, so that a person who has no religious inclination is still defined as being a Jew. Furthermore, to use a label which indicates continental or national origin would be misleading in terms of this special gene pool. Because a Jewish person came from Russia to the United States you would not normally call him a Russo-American or if he came from America you would not say he is an Afro-American. As I have indicated restructuring of identity labels is a problematic undertaking. What Afrocentricity will mean to this process, however, is the coming to terms with national consciousness among the "enia dudu" throughout the world. Such negotiation between a people and their consciousness does not negate nor minimize their essential character. Afrocentricity depoliticizes the concept of race and points the way to the restructuring of identity.

Why have I been writing as if politics and economics are separate matters? Because even though they are both functions of power, they manifest themselves differently. And while it is true that the possessors of one usually possess the other, it is not always the case. There are numerous examples of nations whose politicians are controlled by external economic interests. In fact, our community has seen its share of outside economic control even though politicians have been selected by the community.

One of the most important economic right in the coming decades will be the right to salary. It is very important that we understand the significance of this matter. When one studies, or reads, United States history, it becomes clear that those who owned the land became big capitalists; land is the basis of all wealth. By the time Africans were emancipated the major landholdings had already been taken. Even the land blacks managed to acquire was often taken from them. So in the rise of the spirits it will not be major landholdings that will help us overcome the economic plight that has plagued us. We shall have to fight the contest for salaries. It is increasingly true with whites also that the security of salary is more important than the right to real estate. The large number of people moving into apartments or already living in apartments attests to the declining interest in and ability to buy real estate. We must struggle to gain a foothold in every sector of the American economy. There will continue to be, as there must be, entrepreneurs who will seek to create profits for themselves and positions for others. But the extent of all black owned businesses for the next four decades will be infinitesimal in the total American economy. Our path to economic survival will not be based upon landholdings but owning secure industries, creative breakthroughs in art and music, exploitation of all fields of athletics and salaried positions based on education and talent.

A society much more diversified than we can even now imagine will provide both unlimited opportunity for success in entrepeneurial activities. Given this configuration, our encounter with whites will intensify in those areas where we have traditionally been underemployed, i.e., electronics, corporation management, legal and administrative areas, the medical profession, particularly in the top echelons of medical services, administration of academic institutions, and various positions in the information industry. The white response to this encounter is, as I have pointed out, predictable. There will be subtle moves to evade the inevitable, new white scientists will rise up with fantastic discoveries about black abilities or inabilities, organizations will be formed to promote competence and familiar words will take on unfamiliar meanings among those who are afraid of us. But in the end our Afrocentricity will insure our victory based upon the products, opportunities, and jobs created by our work, sweat, genius, blood, and durability. Quite fortunately we are a persistent people who know that what our prophets predicted must indeed come to pass. And our encounter with Europeans in the economic arena will generate a more cohesive world dedicated to the expression of spirit and soul, and by that, dignity and integrity.

The encounters we experience in various sectors of society will enhance our collective consciousness. We are only now becoming a collective will, the recession of individuality as our main thrust: one brother working as a clerk in a department store, one sister as an accountant in a corporation, one brother in university administration, one sister in chemical research at a national laboratory. instead of one who was usually "the first black to . . . " we have a phalanx which is real not imaginary.

When I was a child in Georgia and we got our first black clerk at the five and ten store, whites would come to the door, stare, then exclaim to other whites while pointing at the trying-to-keep-cool brother, "They are even in here now!" Those were the days of an imagined phalanx. We may not all be preparing ourselves in the same way, but we are *preparing* and that is the key to the rise. The general encounter on a wide range of political, social, and economic issues will contribute to our growing awakeness. We will come to terms with consciousness in spite of the American experience and perhaps *because* of our collective encounter with the European's reaction to our search for human peace. That is why I see the potency of rise as an injection into the world of culture. Consciousness is the first sign of vigor and power. Our rising tide of consciousness will wash all as clean as coal. Already it is a *fait accompli* in American music so will it be in other aspects of American life. It is not to be lamented; it is to be accepted as the natural course of historical maturity where the personal infusion of spirit extends materialism and spirituality to form a people level.

Our knowledge, developed out of necessity, helps to ascertain the political and social direction the nation and world is tending. We know full the distrust the rich white has of the poor white and we also know that the poor whites are constantly struggling to hide their origin. But this is only tangentially our problem, that is, we are affected by the discussions and actions that the rich whites take to frustrate the poor whites but ours is a different problem. Class is significant only as an added dimension to the stratification already present. Because we are surrounded by white cultural styles (and have not been completely overwhelmed) we are aware of communication and social behaviors of whites though we do not participate in those behaviors. Use of terms like "minority," "qualified," "standards," "law and order," and "quality control" when dealing with interracial situations reflect a communication bias often found in white language. It is not stretching the point too far to reiterate that we have been able to tell the direction of national politics by the words that emerge from behind closed doors. American politics is money politics and money determines what shall be spoken in public and what shall not be spoken. The impregnable walls of race dictates that Anglo-Saxons rule the economic sector of the United States. These are differences between non-Anglo-Saxon and Anglo-Saxon wealth. The Jewish rich, department store owners, and media tycoons, can seldom sit at the same tables, that is, share the social clubs or status symbols of the Anglo-Saxon rich.

The rise of Africans in America will have its initial impact on the broad middle of American life and society. Only as a tandem influence, combined with other cultural and political thrusts, will it have an impact on the controllers of the economy. We can only affect the controllers of wealth in the production of their products. Most employees are new peasants. The revolt of the employees is the revolt of the new peasants, when the rise introduces, as surely it must, quite new interpretations of value it will be the collective wills of many segments of society that will react in a major attempt to elevate the employees.

What then is the response of other people likely to be towards Afrocentricity? Certainly there will not be massive participation because Afrocentricity is seen as an antithesis to the architecton set up by Europeans. So the response will be pragmatic, watching the shape of things to come, and deliberate, with good reason for a wait and see attitude. The fact that we will no longer genuflect must not be taken as vindictiveness, it is only another sign of the consciousness that is upon us. Others will find the new epoch to be favorable to their own sense of collective development which will become increasingly like Afrocentricity. Many will embrace it for its humanism and cultural vitality. Each of you know, of course, what we must do.

The Transcendent Process
The transcending action which takes us from the traditional to the

revolutionary consciousness is complex and intriguing. In its most elemental stage, it may be called the eradication, blotting out, of the old and the opening up to the new. We *breakdown* in order to *breakthrough*.

Each person chooses to become Afrocentric; this is the only way to accomplish it. You experience in the *breakdown* a certain tearing away from mental and psychological habits that held you enslaved to Eurocentric concepts. This is a violent process. It is a separation and all separations are violent. We move away from the lifestyles of oppression and victimization. We reject consciousness of oppression. We dispense with attitudes of defeatism. We turn our backs on those negative race behaviors that conceal the manliness and womanliness we possess. We condemn those deviation of symbols and actions which hark back to the slave mentality. Like a dazzling comet our new self radiates to all those in our presence; we become new people.

Breakdown and Breakthrough Strategies

The persistent agitation within western societies that cannot be controlled is bringing on the breakdown of the last remnants of western concepts held by people of African descent. Included in the agitations which lead to the breakdown are: the rise of the Ku Klux Klan, high unemployment of blacks in the cities, white reactionary social consciousness, the paralysis of American cultural institutions, the media distortions of African-Americans and a growing disaffection with government. As to the positive points which encourage the breakdown but point to the breakthrough, they are self-evident in the contemporary age: black interest in African heritage, travel to Africa, rise in the reading level of blacks, involvement in international politics, and the ecological consciousness among blacks reflecting our return to our African spiritual base.

The following outline may help you achieve your own breakthrough of Afrocentricity. The procedure outlined here will provide you with a start toward self-liberation and collective conscious will out of which comes our own national imperative.

Breakdown	*Breakthrough*
slave name	choose African name
defeatist notions	victorious thought
can't do attitudes	confident attitudes
love of other cultures first	love of own culture first
negative race behaviors	positive race behaviors
consciousness of oppression	consciousness of victory
slouch posture	erect posture
dress European	reflect own motifs in dress

blind religious obedience	personal spiritual growth
disrespect for people	respect for people
incompetence	excellence
historical discontinuity	historical continuity
relate all to Europe	relate all to Africa
visit only European shrines	visit African shrines
pathetic	proud

The columns show how one can dispense with some attitudes and replace them with others; it is like the process of decolonizing and liberating the mind. Afrocentricity is a liberating ideology. A person who chooses to live an Afrocentric life will always transcend the mundane attitudes. To be Afrocentric is to be in touch with one's ultimate reality in every way.

Throughout the period of breakdown, it may be necessary for you to share your transcendence with a brother or sister because the process of breaking down is painful. We tried it in the 1960's to shock the slave out of the person only to discover that the slave merely left for a while only to reappear and possess the person almost as firmly as before. This time our aim is to allow each person to manage his/her own change. We do not want total catastrophe or collapse, but we do want a cleansing. This cleansing will be based upon each of us searching out the deviations within us, the European interpretations, the misreading of history and events and the elimination of those negatives.

There are no reasons for lamentations, there are only challenges to be fulfilled. We have already achieved more than any other recently oppressed people on earth; the future belongs to the Afrocentric cadre of 250,000 who shall exemplify the most positive elements of our will and determination. In every historical epoch, the spiritual and cultural bearing stratum has centered in one particular people. Today, some of the most revolutionary thinkers are children of heroic Africans who came to America as enslaved prisoners of war.

When the breakthrough occurs for an individual, it is manifest in *constructing, enabling,* and *liberating* roles. For example, the creation of growth opportunities for others by communicating new concepts of power, love relationships, and ideological represent a construction task. Enablers help others take control of their minds and bodies through an Afrocentric lifestyle. And when one seeks to remove all vestiges of enslavement, all accoutrements of victimization from all African people, she is liberating.

Thought and Action

Neither action nor thought is good in and of itself, each must be accompanied by the other. The world has seen too much abuse brought about because of one element without the other. I believe in practical involvement. In effect, we begin with one transcendent element. We have identified three main roles for transcendentalists: (1) constructing, (2) enabling, and (3) liberating.

As a practical guide to action, the three roles are paired with activities which reflect our existence. The three roles explained are as follows:

Constructing. Changing concepts and symbols so that they become more consistent with the Afrocentric point of view.

Enabling. Managing the breakdown of the old order so that dependent needs are met and filled by people becoming more self-reliant.

Liberating. Developing alternative lifestyles and relationships and the use of Afrocentricity to secure freedom.

The activity areas are as follows:

family	housing
land use	cities
technology	religion
government	crime and prisons
economics	work
energy	education
transport	health

Any combination of a transcendent role and one of these activity areas will produce a changed frame of reference. If, for example, a person chose the transcendent role "enabling" from the list, the activity area could be any one in the list. For example, if we had enabling and work, it would mean acting to encourage more awareness on the part of police. It could mean enabling a factory to create more humanistic employment opportunities or the assumption of collective ownership by the people. Whatever it means to you, you must take courage and do it.

The Afrocentric future will be built upon the foundation maintained by the giants who live inside you. Your knowledge, your condition, your vision belong to all of us. Therefore, this is your book, read it and pass it on to others, we have a job to do.

Innovation and Tradition

The two fundamental aspects of the Afrocentric project are *innovation* and *tradition*. Both are essential to the historical process of humanizing the world. The generation of the new, the novel, is basic to the advancement of cultural ideas but also is the maintenance of the traditional. Innovation permits us, indeed requires us, the promotion of new themes and designs founded on the traditional motifs.

Afrocentricity is the operative theory upon which we hang our innovation and tradition. As I have contended, there is nothing more correct, more innovative, more rooted in tradition, than the centrality of our own historical experiences.

The principal paths to a practical cultural project is through the Afrocentric door. Afrocentricity is not Africanity. It is not the mere existence of the African person as an African person but rather the active, self-conscious advancement of the humanizing motif in every sector of society. It is an architect appealing to traditional classic motifs in the generation of the new and modern. It is the economist examining and applying the relevant and positive traditions of Africans to the economy. It is the political scientist and politician seeing in the traditional the possibilities for dynamic change.

Being born on the continent of African ancestry and with African historical experiences makes one an African; it does not make one Afrocentric. As a house is not a home, Africanity is not Afrocentricity. Being black does not make you Afrocentric. Nevertheless, Afrocentricity builds upon several intellectual foundations such as Garveyism, Kawaida, and Négritude. Yet, without the genius of those ways of viewing the African presence and reality, Afrocentricity could never have been. Quite correctly, there is no other truth more necessary for the intellectual, political, economic, and cultural advancement of the world than African people immersing themselves in the waters of a cultural rebirth. This is the hard truth of history, and the only real lesson we need to learn for the total liberation of ourselves and our children.

The rejection of European particularism as universal is the first stage of our coming intellectual struggle. Five hundred years of constant propaganda, cultural exploitation, information distortion, and physical annihilation have left the African world shocked out of its own historical reality and purpose in the world. The names of ancient cities and geographical phenomena have been changed. Eight thousand years of African civilization have disappeared from the imagination of most of our writers and scientists. European aggression has been equated with intelligence and Africa reels from the effects of this aggression unable to shake the theoretical, political, economic, or cultural chains.

The colonization of the world by the Europeans was not an act of innocence. It was not a charitable act by any fantasy of the imagination or by any objective analysis. Entire cosmologies were dumped on the trash heap of a crusading European ideology that meant to plunder, not only the people's land and bodies, but their minds as well (Redding, 1950). The liberation of the minds of African peoples will be a tougher battle than the eradication of settler regimes.

Rivers, streams, mountains, and lakes bear evidence of the disregard with which the European settlers considered our ancestors. These symbols attest to the thorough nature of the attempt to brainwash African minds. Fortunately, the program of distortion has never been completely successful. Afrocentricity as a science and method seeks to change the way we refer to ourselves and our history. It dictates the restoration of the entire African cultural project. It places brakes on our intellectual and theoretical disfranchisement.

Culture is not a narrow term. Consequently, the Afrocentric cultural project is a wholistic plan to reconstruct and develop every dimension of the African world from the standpoint of Africa as subject rather than object. Culture is the totalization of the historical, artistic, economic, and spiritual aspects of a people's lifestyle. Afrocentricity assumes that African government officials will become conscious of the centrality of Africa in their deliberations, that writers will seek to influence the African people, that we re-connect, in our minds, ancient Nubia and Kemet to the rest of Africa, that we speak on every subject and every issue affecting the world. While our hospitality has been our greatest weakness, it is also our greatest weakness, it is also our greatest human strength in the humanizing project.

When I call for Afrocentricity, I am also calling for a new historiography founded on African aspirations, visions, and concepts. The search is not for a naive nationalism nor a superficial socialism but rather a deep, self-conscious, positive relationship with our own experiences. This is no easy project; it takes boldness, intelligence, and planning. Such a project, Africa-centered as it will be, means that no one anywhere in the world would be allowed to abuse, exploit, or harm African people without our collective wrath. Those who have committed and commit massive crimes against African people cannot be allowed to go free without the rebuke and trial of the people.

When European travellers in the sixteenth–nineteenth centuries came in contact wiht Africans, Native Americans, and Asians, they often wrote in their diaries like Captain Cook of Britain wrote when the native Hawaiians came out to meet his ship with fruits and flowers, "The natives think that we are gods." In Africa, these travellers always recorded that "Africans were child-like." What they meant was that our ancestors were civilized, hospitable, and open to strangers. World history teaches us to be suspicious while retaining the culture bequeathed by generations.

We overseas Africans have a keen sense of the need to reclaim the continent itself. It is a historical connection, not to be taken lightly, and with this Pan-African ideology, Africa can redeem itself. Of all the continents, African had often seemed the most disconcerted by its children who have been scattered over the globe. A great part of this has to do with the confusion of the children of Africa themselves. Often detached and isolated from Africa they assume new identities and become doubly lost, zombies in the midst of stone and steel cities of the Americas. Yet it is imperative that the African in Colombia who speaks Spanish, the African in Brazil who speaks Portuguese, the African in Martinique who speaks French, and the African in Jamaica who speaks English be brought into this cultural project. Just as the Australian European living thousands of miles away from Europe participates in the European project; the African must be brought into the cultural project of Africa whether in Cuba or the United States, Haiti or Nicaragua, Mexico or Colombia.

One day on the continent of Africa we will see an Afrocentric univeristy with its curriculum geared towards the Pan-African world as central not peripheral to knowledge. We must vow, an Ogunic iron vow, if necessary, that we will neither tolerate nor allow any attack on African people. This means that no other African person should participate in the exploitation of African people.

The task is for the lion-hearted. It requires discipline and devotion to the African cultural project on several levels. We must change the vocabulary that some Africans and most Europeans adopt in reference to us. There were no "warlike" people in Africa, at least, no more than the French or English or Germans were warlike when they invaded Africa. Normally, if an ethnic group or nation defended itself it was labeled by the invaders as "warlike." We reject that outright. The words "Hottentot," "Bushmen," and "Pygmy" must be dispensed with as pejoratives. The *Khoi, San,* and *Twa* people did not and do not call themselves by the European pejoratives; neither should the Afrocentric writer. A colonized mind is always on the verge of menticide, the destruction of the minds, the suicide of minds. We can achieve the humanizing mission of the earth by remembering that the idea for culture and civilization first went down the Nile from the interior of Africa. Our anteriority is only significant because it re-affirms for us that if we once organized complex civilizations all over the continent of Africa, we can take those traditions and generate more advanced ideas. Let the artist imagine, let the scientists expand, let the priests see visions, let the writers be free to create, and let an Afrocentric revolution be born!

Njia: The Way

Quarter One

1. This is The Way that came to Molefi in America.
2. The person who wishes death, attains it.
3. The person who wishes life, attains it.
4. All else is neither guidance nor religion.
5. Feeling is before belief and to everyone who feels is given belief.
6. A religion of the head brings dogma; feeling brings life.
7. Rejoice in The Way because it is right to rejoice in happiness.
8. The Way is not contradictory to Hinduism, Judaism, Christianity, Islam, Yoruba, or any other way of peace and power; it is complementary.
9. It comes last in the revelations; thus it builds upon previous foundations.
10. The Way is rooted in historical experiences and exists because it is spoken.
11. All things that are, exist through speech. Without speech there is Nothing.
12. Whatever a person speaks has reality to that person.
13. It may be sane or insane but it is reality. This is the power of speech.
14. No spoken word can be ignored. Once it is spoken, it exists.
15. The Way achieves nothing for you. You achieve all things through your own efforts.
16. Some will say, "we cannot do so and so." This is an aberration.
17. Some will say, "we will do it at some other time." This is procrastination.

18. Neither aberrations nor procrastinations are worthy of The Way. Whatever is of life can be done if you have a will to do it.
19. Whatever is of life should be done immediately.
20. In risk one finds the edge of The Way. It is the beginning of liberation.
21. Solidarity with truth is the only solidarity that matters.
22. One needs no work, no power but truth, spoken and upheld, to defeat evil.
23. Where there is truth, evil is dissipated.
24. The liberation of the weak is the task of the strong. Hearts that are strong should comfort the weak. This is the truth.
25. Never listen to those who scoff at your ancestors. They understand neither history nor truth.

Quarter Two

1. Honor to the ancestors is indivisible. Some will say honor your parents. The Way says honor all your ancestors.
2. During the afflictions of Abibiman, many were slaves but all were royalty. This is the truth.
3. Those who seek attention, do so at their own peril. The eyes of their enemies see them first.
4. Be wise in everything that you do for you never know who seeks to do you harm or who seeks to do you good.
5. They who smile may also wear a frown.
6. Have no illusions, build no mansions of fantasy. Do only that which is found in The Way.
7. If you have no illusions you can never be called ignorant; with illusions you will never be wise.
8. A wise person speaks carefully and with truth for every word that passes between one's teeth is meant for something.
9. No child belongs only to the parents. All children are yours; treat them kindly and with great respect.
10. In the midst of confusion keep your heart simple because there is nothing that cannot be understood.
11. What appears complex at one time will reveal itself to be exceedingly simple the next time.
12. Patient is not procrastination. The wise act with truth, the procrastinator does not act even with truth.
13. Action is virtuous; but you must act wisely. This is the truth.
14. It is better to be an apprentice briefly than a disciple forever. Therefore, learn what you can from your teacher and become one yourself.

15. If you follow what is good in you, The Way will be satisfied.
16. Seek unity. It is natural that human beings should cooperate.
17. Plan judiciously to achieve cooperation. Do not disdain others who are committed to unity.
18. The Way encourages every person to become a part of a collective harmony. In togetherness, there is strength and beauty.
19. Unity is like a flower, its glory is its fullness.
20. The person who disrupts the harmony of human beings must know what she/he is doing.
21. Harmony is only beauty when it is based upon The Way.
22. Some will counsel you to seek harmony at any cost, do not heed them.
23. The Way that came to me is how it is and how it must be for Abibiman.
24. Some would try to bring contradictions but it is because they neither understand who they are nor where they came from.
25. Free yourself. This is the truth.

Quarter Three

1. Lies are insidious. They grow into human relationships like dandelions. They sometimes look good but they are hard to root out.
2. You are an historic people. The Way was opened to your ancestors. It is passed on to you, written in your very walk.
3. Your parents endured trials and tribulations but have left a strong progeny.
4. When you know you are right, say it loud. Never be afraid to speak up for The Way.
5. Those who are afraid of The Way will be fearful of life itself. The Way is life.
6. You must never doubt The Way; it is sown into your very existence.
7. Love is more than a word; it is more than a feeling. To love someone is to live for someone.
8. You demonstrate your love by your commitment. Be careful that you do not use words meaninglessly.
9. If you should see a person asking for food, share your food for in sharing your food you spread The Way.
10. Whatever your position in life, you are never greater nor less than The Way.
11. Respect each other; greet one another as you pass by for you never know when you will pass by your mother.
12. Do not be pained by little things; they are only irritants.
13. Keep your eyes on the large things; they can do you harm or good.
14. Never allow general accusations to be taken personally by you.

15. When you have seen The Way, you must discuss it with those who are blind.
16. Your feet carry you up the same way that Abraham, Ishmael, Jacob, Jesus, Mohammad, Candhi, and King carried them.
17. Act natural wherever you are.
18. If you are for real, you will be praised. If you are a fake, you will be cursed. This is the truth.
19. A person who is dissatisfied with her/himself will spread dissatisfaction to her/his friends.
20. Your enemies will call you names the very opposite of what your friends call you.
21. Do not allow your natural compassion and kindness to beguile you. Be vigilant.
22. Seek only to maintain your dignity and your character will be strengthened each day.
23. As it was in the affliction of Abibiman, valleys become hills and hills become valleys; so it shall be for you.
24. Give praise to your ancestors who established religious fellowships in A.B.A. 170.
25. Teach your children strength that they may continue the heritage you have received.

Quarter Four

1. Fight those who with malice initiate violent actions against you. If you are responsible for violent acts against your brother or sister, you will be harshly treated by those who follow The Way.
2. Any person who violently attacks an elder man or woman, a pregnant woman, or a child will be harshly treated by those who follow The Way.
3. Right actions stems from right hearts.
4. You are meant to be a sign for the world. Your spirit is the Spirit of Humanity.
5. When you are in someone else's home, follow the lead of your host.
6. When you greet another say, "Peace, to you belongs freedom." When another greets you say, "Peace, and to our children."
7. There is nothing more precious than an honest friendship.
8. Never allow evil to burn in your hearts. Go to the one who offends you and lay the matter on the line.
9. When Nat Turner met in the woods with his bloods, they pledged themselves to liberty. This is the true pledge.

10. Chit-chat is not productive it only produces false images of ourselves and others. Learn to speak authoritatively.
11. Defend all misunderstood persons, this will make you a mediator.
12. In The Way, the person who mediates finds peace.
13. You must struggle against all forms of hypocrisy; those who fail to expose hypocrisy cannot be called lovers of freedom.
14. Respect the high shrines and observe the high days. This will give you strength.
15. Remember the high days as a test of your discipline. For if you are able to keep the high days you will surely be able to overcome evil.
16. Never mistreat a friend for the true friend is a rare find. A person who has ten true friends is both rich and wise.
17. Consider the raccoon who washes before he eats; his example is a piece of gold.
18. The Way is always illuminated by those who have travelled it before you; so be not afraid of its turns because light is always around the next curve.
19. Extend kindness to every child in the anticipation that kindness will become a universal blessing.
20. Racism is despicable; you should neither practice it nor allow it to be practiced.
21. Honorable is the person who exposes the despicable ones. This is The Truth.
22. When DuBois was young he dedicated himself to uncovering racism and won himself a place in human hearts.
24. DuBois is a worthwhile example. The person who models his or her life after DuBois will find a place in the assembly of freedom lovers.
25. You must be cautious around strangers; they may not be friends nor angels.

Quarter Five

1. Respect yourself and others will wonder who you are. Despise yourself and others will wonder what are you.
2. Do not fail to act courteously toward all people. You never know when you will need others.
3. Never vandalize what others have built with their genius.
4. Study history. You are the center of what you study.
5. Every child should be encouraged to learn everything. This is The Way.
6. Never despise the person who writes books. The books that are written are a part of humanity.

7. Women and men deserve equal respect; they are equally the source of your historic strength and courage.
8. Remember that a clear sense of identity is hard to contradict. This is the truth.
9. Organize your thoughts in order to be able to organize communities. Without unity all tasks seem impossible.
10. There is but one ideology—to do justice and to have mercy.
11. Listen to the elders and mark their words. They have travelled the path before you. And what they say is golden.
12. Visit the elders, sit at their feet and have no fear. They are your wisdom.
13. When you become disturbed by some problem, take a good look at yourself, and you will see the solution.
14. Study David Walker who gave power to
15. Henry Highland Garnet who in his youth
16. inspired Reverdy Ransom whose spirit touched
17. Frederick Douglass who spread wisdom
18. to Bishop Henry McNeal Turner who anticipated
19. W.E.B. DuBois
20. who influenced Booker T. Washington who inspired
21. Marcus Garvey who
22. gave us Malcolm X and Martin Luther King and Stokely Carmichael and Maulana Karenga.
23. So study these brothers and all of those who follow in their steps.
24. And as you read these brothers, study Sojourner Truth and Harriet Tubman and Ida B. Wells, and Fannie Lou Hamer and Rosa Parks, and Angela Davis and Coretta King.
25. These souls constitute a great host of warrior-lovers; study tehm and walk in their courage.

Quarter Six
1. Remember Kwanzaa.
2. These words came to Karenga in the year 351 A.B.A.: "These are the Nguzo Saba. Seek *UMOJA* for it is to seek unity. Strive for *Kujichagulia* and determine your destiny. Honor *Ujima* by collective work and responsibility. Apply *Ujamaa*, collective economics, to your life. Maintain *Nia*, purpose, in all your actions. Respective creatively, *Kuumba*, as you respect your parents. Keep *Imani*, faith, with each other. These seven principles are always in The Way of truth."
3. When you have achieved Nguzo Saba, teach others, for we are one blood.

4. Add to the Nguzo Saba, *Uhuru* and *Salaama* for freedom and peace belong to each of you.
5. And Karenga received the words of Kwanzaa in the same year as the Nguzo Saba. This was before his captivity.
6. "Kwanzaa is the celebration of life. During it shall no blood be found lying, stealing nor fighting. It is a time for reflection on the Nguzo Saba."
7. It is a time of rededication to just struggle. It is a time for the young and old to be happy. Celebrate Kwanzaa and rejoice for you are a historic people.
8. Karenga wrote these words, "Kwanzaa means first fruits. We celebrate harvest. There is a harvest of food, there is a harvest of love, there is a harvest of good deeds. There is a harvest of friendship. We are a first harvest people."
9. When you celebrate Kwanzaa do it with other bloods who have read The Way.
10. The first day of Kwanzaa is December 26. All preparations for the Kwanzaa table must be made on December 25.
11. Children should participate in all phases of preparation. Given them responsibility for the cloths, which should be red, black and green. These are the historic colors.
12. Fresh fruits, green vegetables, African artifacts, histories of the people's struggle against racism, and flowers should be judiciously placed around the seven candles of Kwanzaa.
13. On each night of Kwanzaa the eldest member of the family will provide a lesson on one of the Nguzo Saba.
14. The night of *Imani*, the seventh night shall be a night of fun and sharing. Share only those things you make with your own hands. Teach this well and you will be fortunate.
15. In everything you do, be mindful of your example to others. Teach well.
16. On July 3 of every year the beginning again is remembered by fasting for twelve hours. As you fast, teach each other.
17. This is the rememberance of twenty souls who came to America in the first year of the beginning again.
18. Do not be afraid to speak to those bloods who refuse to fast. They are neither conscious nor on The Way. Teach them.
19. And when you have fasted and remembered the beginning again, pledge yourself to help and comfort each other.
20. The fast should end with the singing of Spirituals left to us by many millions gone.

21. Other ways will be written, but know that This Way belongs to you!
22. Study nature.
23. The price of strength is to be attached by those who are weaker.
24. The word that Karenga received while in captivity was to never allow the world to impose upon you. This is the truth.
25. Honor those who are in exile for false reasons they are your conscience.

Quarter Seven
1. Learn to write well and you will be heard.
2. Be kind to all people but never be a pushover.
3. Refuse to be dogmatic in all things except The Way.
4. The Way is neither poetry nor is it prose, yet it is both.
5. The Way encompasses all parts, and honors the great messengers.
6. The revelation of The Way is pure. This is the truth.
7. Because it is true The Way travels through the air faster than any space vehicle. Truth is indivisible everywhere.
8. All lovers should give praise and honor to each other.
9. Avoid violence, both physical and psychological, and treat each other as friends.
10. Gentleness is the first law of love.
11. If you must separate, do it with all gentleness; otherwise separation will be more painful.
12. Remain sober and you will always know what is happening to you.
13. Avoid excessive use of intoxicants; they impair more than vision.
14. Meet together and discuss The Way. You will find a community of truth is the source of strength.
15. The Lord of our ancestors reigns over the universe and guides us as we walk in The Way. This is the truth.
16. Give praise to all spirits, and live in harmony with all living spirits.
17. There is no way more perfect for you than The Way derived from your own historical experiences. Learn this well and teach others.
18. The person who strays away from the source is unrooted and is like dust blown about by the wind.
19. Embrace your ancestors for they have embraced you.
20. You are the miracle of The Way, an expressed symbol to the survival of spirit.
21. Anger toward those who do injustice and tolerate oppression is natural, but never allow it to rule you.
22. Be no one's slave, neither have slaves yourself. Fight with those who fight against servitude.

23. Honor the paths of Krishna, Moses, Jesus, Mohammad, Anokye and Confucius, they are also revelations of light.
24. Altruism is not to be expected, therefore express surprise when it is shown to you.
25. You are what you make of yourself, never what others made you.

Quarter Eight
1. Remake yourself through discipline, exercise and work. You will discover your own worth.
2. Surround your environment with beauty. Natural beauty is the best of all.
3. Sing the songs of your ancestors and find wisdom. This is the truth.
4. Teach your children music and dance for they are the first and second canons of harmony.
5. Respect the circle, it has neither ends nor corners.
6. Stand on your past and reach toward the future, for to you belongs the future.
7. Your ancestors crossed the sea in a million ships each containing your religion, culture and wisdom.
8. They planted the soil and left their seed and blood in the harvest.
9. Rivers were bridged, mountains were tunneled, highways were constructed, rail lines were laid, and cities were erected by their hands.
10. Your ancestors, of all people, were selected for a unique lesson to humanity.
11. Written in your spirit is the integrity of wholeness.
12. Remember the crossing for it led to the beginning again.
13. The men and women who came created the community from which you came.
14. They are the roots and you are the branches.
15. Against seemingly impossible odds, they maintained families, reared children, and passed on the elements of your soul.
16. The land they walked sung their praises and raised trees in their honor.
17. Remember that in their pain the oak, hickory and magnolia shouted in ecstasy.
18. These bloods, who knew two worlds, made history a sacred tradition.
19. As the sun is over the clouds you shall be over your enemies if you study The Way and keep the high days.
20. Study the clouds from below and above and rise above circumstances.
21. The high shrines are commemorative and instructive visit them and contemplate the past and the future.

22. Every Abibiman should visit Jamestown. it is the place the earth was first touched in America.
23. All that was touched before was unimportant to your history and culture. This is the truth.
24. Tuskegee's ground is immortal. Walk carefully on its campus and you will feel the presence of souls.
25. Plan your actions well, you will surprise even yourself with your success.

Quarter Nine

1. Beware of what you eat because you so easily become what you eat.
2. Have compassion for all mistreated persons. Stand strongly with them and you will find happiness.
3. Make a habit of your history. Be knowledgeable and you shall be free. This is the truth.
4. Practice all the arts for you are an artistic people Humanize and liberalize your surroundings through your art.
5. Give deference to the poor and you shall be rewarded.
6. Struggle constantly against those who discriminate among people on the basis of color and you will walk the way of honor.
7. Knowledge follows humility.
8. When you feel the wind you are feeling the Presence. Therefore, never ask, where is the Presence? It is everywhere.
9. Rhythm is the primary fact of life. Participate in the rhythm of the universe and sense happiness.
10. When brother struggles against brother, enemies will gather their spoils. This is the truth.
11. Kariamu received the words of Mfundalai in A.B.A. 352.
12. "You are the descendants of the first people. Mfundalai came with the beginning of the people; it was perfected in you in America. It is the edge of ecstacy, it is the point of joy, it is the expectation of beauty, and it is the consummation of poetic energies. Mfundalai should be sought in the right places."
13. And Kariamu received these words in A.B.A. 353. "The Mfundalai rite shall proclaim the coming to be of the man in the boy and the woman in the girl."
14. "At thirteen years of age every child shall be required to participate in the Mfundalai rite of the coming of age."
15. "The child shall recite from The Way, interpret the recitation, and apply it to the life of a messenger."

16. "The Mfundalai rite shall be held only in the presence of friends of the family."
17. "Younger children should occupy the chief seats in every Mfundalai rite. They are the gems which shall shine in the future."
18. At the completion of the rite the child becomes a responsible part of the people. A child who has completed Mfundalai has completed the first part of The Way.
19. Keep the rites and remember their origins.
20. Remember the day when your blood and skin left the earth and crossed the waters and touched the earth. That day is the beginning again.
21. It is your first year so teach your children to mark time back and forth from the beginning again.
22. The beginning again is the most sacred day, you must reflect upon the meaning of your presence in America on that day.
23. Your fast should be done in quietude, not with boasting.
24. The high shrines of the real messengers should be visited during this time.
25. In Harlem and Watts, at both ends of America, you will find many messengers. Rejoice and be glad.

Quarter Ten

1. The person is a great messenger who teaches you about yourself in the spirit of power and strength.
2. Learn well everything that challenges you; you will overcome all obstacles in your path.
3. Contemplate the expansiveness of the sky and understand its meaning to your people and you shall be called wise.
4. The person of truth stands erect; the person of falsehood droops his/her shoulders in disgrace.
5. Never accommodate evil thoughts against one another. You so easily become what you think.
6. Be careful how you reveal yourself to the treacherous. Treachery will misuse openness.
7. Resist those who would enslave your body or your mind. This is the truth.
8. You are a proud people. Do not allow your pride to blind you to the inadequacies which you possess.
9. A person who kills your brothers and sisters today cannot become your friend tomorrow.

10. The messenger Elijah Muhammad once said, "The enemy is a hypocrite who will try to change his enmity to friendship overnight."
11. Learn to conserve your wealth so that you may be able to help your children. This is the truth.
12. The Way teaches that you should be generous to all causes which seek to enhance quality of human life.
13. Respect the great books and teach your children to respect them as well.
14. Give praise to the soul of the universe.
15. When you provide sustenance to your physical body, do so in great reverence.
16. Protect your body.
17. Be not disturbed by your enemies.
18. Pour libations and sing the songs of your ancestors for strength.
19. Speak only the truth as your parents taught you from the beginning again.
20. Give thought to kindness and do kindness. This is The Way.
21. Your power is in your faith. Keep it and pass it to other bloods.
22. Honor The Way.
23. Honor all who memorize The Way.
24. This book is only the first relevation in America. You test its authenticity by living its principles. This is the truth.

Glossary

A.B.A.
> The time after 1619 when African landed in Virginia as indentured servants. After the Beginning Again.

Afrology
> The science or study of all modalities related to people of African descent from an Afrocentric perspective.

B.B.A.
> The time before 1619. Before the Beginning Again.

Chaka
> Legendary Zulu king who introduced warfare and administrative innovations later adopted by European armies. 19th century.

Classical Music
> African-American Jazz based on African polyrhythms and syncopation.

Deviation
> Any action, word, or thought which does not adhere to the Afrocentric perspective.

Ebonics
> A language spoken in the United States by African-Americans which uses many English words but is based on African syntactic elements and sense modalities.

Guillen, Nicolas
> The Afro-Cuban poet laureate of the Cuban revolution.

Imani
> Kiswahili word for faith.

Jamestown
First permanent residence of Africans in Virginia.

Kawaida
Afro-American religion and ideology founded by Maulana Karenga in the 1960's in Los Angeles.

Kujichagulia
Kiswahili word for self-determination.

Kuumba
Kiswahili word for creativity.

Lake Bosumtwi
Sacred lake of the Akan near Kumasi, Ghana.

Menes
African king who united upper (southern) Egypt with lower (northern) Egypt and established the first dynasty in 3300 B.C.

Mfundalai
A philosophy of African aesthetics developed by choreographer-writer, Kariamu Welsh.

Mfundalai Shairi Dansi
The name given to classical African-American Dance which is based on Afrocentric movements and physiques. It combines historical, poetic, and aesthetic elements in accordance to the discipline of mfundalai.

Mzilikazi
The nineteenth-century Zulu king who extended the influence of the Zulu empire and culture by spreading its power North and East forming the great Matebele kingdom.

Négritude
A dynamic literary movement led by French writing Africans in France in the 1930's. Leopold Senghor, Aime Cesaire, Alioune Diop, Leon Damas, and Jacques Rabemananjara were the leaders of the movement.

Nia
Kiswahili word for purpose.

Njia
A family celebration based on the deification of ancestors. Also word which means "the way" ub Kiswahili language.

Nommo
The generative and productive power of the spoken word.

Nzingha
Legendary 17th century Angolan queen who fought against the Portuguese. She swore a vengeance against them for their destruction of her society and waited for twenty years to fight them.

Obatala
   Yoruba deity of reproduction.
Oduduwa
   Founder of the great Yoruba nation.
Ogun
   Yoruba deity of iron and creativity.
Orishas
   The deities of the Yoruba religion.
Oshogbo
   A sacred city of the Yoruba.
Oshun
   Yoruba goddess; one of Shango's wives identified with fertility.
Quilombismo
   Afro-Brazilian ideology founded by Abdias do Nascimento for the liberation of sixty million Africans. Based on the free kingdom of Quilombo established by revolutionary Africans under the leadership of Zumbi. Quilombismo is a systematic nationalism.
Shango
   Yoruba god of thunder, storm and fire.
Simple
   A character created by Langston Hughes to ridicule racism.
Thebes
   African city which was the first city in the world, originally called Nowe or No.
Ujamaa
   Kiswahili word for cooperative economics.
Ujima
   Kiswahili word for collective work and responsibility.
Umoja
   Kiswahili word for unity.
Yaa Asantewaa
   Nineteenth-century Asante queen mother who led women and children to repel the British forces at Kumasi.

References

Asante M. (1987) *The Afrocentric Idea*. Philadelphia: Temple University Press.

Asante, M. (1978) "Systematic Nationalism." *Journal of Black Studies*, September.

Azikiwe, Nnamdi (1970) *My Odyssey*. New York: Prager.

Ben-Jochannon (1972) *Black Man of the Nile*. New York: Alkebu-Lan Books.

Diop, Cheikh Anta (1974) *The African Origin of Civilization*. New York: Lawrence Hill and Company.

Diop, Cheikh Anta (1978) *The Cultural Unity of Black Africa*. Chicago: Third World Press.

Du Bois, Shirley Graham (1971) *His Day is Marching On: A Memoir of W.E.B. Du Bois*. Philadelphia: Lippincott.

Du Bois, W.E.B. (1961) *The Souls of Black Folk*. New York: Fawcett World Library.

Garvey, Amy Jacques (1969) *The Philosophy and Opinions of Marcus Garvey*. New York: Atheneum.

Jackson, John G. (1970) *Introduction to African Civilization*. New York: Citadel Press.

James, George (1976) *Stolen Legacy*. San Francisco: Richardson Associates.

Karenga, R. (1979) "Afro-American Values." A speech given at the Center for Positive Thought in Buffalo, New York.

Karenga, R. (1978) *Essays in Struggle*. San Diego: Kawaida Publications.

King, Martin Luther, Jr. (1964) *Why We Can't Wait*. New York: New American Library.

Madhubuti, Haki (1978) *Enemies: The Clash of Races*. Chicago: Third World Press.

Maglanbayan, Shawna (1972) *Garvey, Lumumba, Malcolm: Black Nationalist Separatists*. Chicago: Third World Press.

Moore, Carlos (1972) *Were Marx and Engles White Racists?* Chicago: Institute of Positive Education.

Padmore, George (1972) *Africa and World Peace*. London: Frank Cass.

Partington, Paul G. (1977) *W.E.B. Du Bois: A Bibliography of His Published Writings*. Whittier, California: Partington.

Redding, J. Saunders (1950) *They Came in Chains: Americans from Africa*. New York: Doubleday.

Stuckey, Sterling (1972) *The Ideological Origins of Black Nationalism*. Boston: Beacon Press.

Walker, David (1965) *An Appeal to the Colored Citizens of the World in One Continual Cry*, edited by Aptheker, Herbert. New York: Humanities.

Washington, Booker T. (1899) *The Future of the American Negro*. Boston: Small, Maynard.

Welsh, K. (1978) *Textured Women, Beetle Sticks and Cowrie Shells*. Buffalo: Amulefi.

Williams, Chancellor (1974) *The Destruction of Black Civilization*. Chicago: Third World Press.